# Seven Came Through

# Seven Came Through

## RICKENBACKER'S FULL STORY

By

## Captain Edward V. Rickenbacker

WITH AN INTRODUCTION BY

## W. L. White

Author of *They Were Expendable*

Doubleday, Doran and Company, Inc.

GARDEN CITY, NEW YORK

*1943*

PRINTED AT THE *Country Life Press*, GARDEN CITY, N. Y., U. S. A.

*This book is manufactured under wartime conditions in conformity with all government regulations controlling the use of paper and other materials.*

CL

COPYRIGHT, 1943
BY DOUBLEDAY, DORAN & COMPANY, INC.

43-51079
Oct 2'78

# Contents

# Introduction

THE FIRST TIME I saw Eddie Rickenbacker was during the early days of the New Deal, when he appeared before a congressional committee which was delving into the air lines. Whether he appeared of his own accord or was subpoenaed by the Forces of Righteousness I don't remember, nor even what the argument was about.

I only remember dreary hours of cautious palaver and prepared statements from chubby, neatly barbered little men who had all arrived with brief cases. Then all of a sudden they announced Eddie Rickenbacker, and he came striding across the room, towering over the little guys.

Then he began to talk, and you could see why he hadn't brought any brief case. Because he was laying it out to them cold, just as he believed it, let the chips fall where they may, all of it with the vehemence of a great earnestness, without benefit of statistics nor encumbered by unnecessary grammar. Some of the little men with brief cases were allied with Eddie and at times they seemed perturbed as to what he might be going to say—timorous lest some of Eddie's chips fly in the wrong direction, as I have no doubt a few of them did.

Because what we had there was not just a man, but a primitive force of nature which, with the weight of its great sincerity, swept everything before it. When he had finished, he did not go on talking, as most of the others had, but stopped and left the room, and for the rest of the day nothing the plump little men with the brief cases said seemed to matter.

So let's examine this elemental force which has made him a dynamic figure not only in two wars, but in the two intervening decades. His parents came from the German-speaking cantonments of Switzerland, but he himself was born in Columbus, Ohio, in 1890.

His father died when he was twelve. The day after the funeral he went down to the Columbus Glass Company and talked himself into a job by saying he was fourteen. That was the end of his schooling. He worked twelve hours a night, six nights a week, and turned his weekly $3.50 pay check over intact to his mother. Presently he got a better job ($6 a week) in a foundry. Then to a shoe factory at $10, and at last to a garage, where he learned the little there was then to know about the horseless carriage. He took correspondence courses in engineering and in 1910 began winning automobile races. Four years later he had pushed a Blitzen Benz to the unbelievable world's record of one hundred and thirty-four miles per hour. When war came he was the ace of Army staff drivers, but after driving General Pershing just once, everybody agreed his talents had a higher usefulness and he went into aviation, then an obscure branch of the signal corps, where he soon picked up the tricks of the Lafayette Escadrille, and when war ended he was America's premier ace with nineteen decorations for bravery and an official box score of twenty-two German planes and four balloons. After various business ventures he finally found his place in the thirties as a leader in the air-transport industry.

Through the decades he has retained public respect not solely because of his great earnestness, but because he speaks out only where he knows what he is talking about.

It was thus when in 1925 he thundered out in defense of General Billy Mitchell: "It's a crime against posterity! The nation will pay for their selfishness! Not perhaps in this generation, but in that of the boys who are growing up today, or their sons. A qualified air service is the life insurance of our national integrity."

And again, when the air-mail contracts were canceled and untrained, inexperienced Army pilots were ordered to fly the mails, Eddie roared forth that it was "legalized murder."

So now for this present book. No man of this living generation has seen death more closely and more often than Eddie Rickenbacker. There were those early crashes on the speedway and the close shaves when he brought down the twenty-two German planes and four German balloons. He has learned to look the Old Fellow right back in the eye, as one man to another, returning his steady gaze. He is never flustered. That night in Febru-

ary 1941 when rescuers crowded around the wrecked
air liner in the pine forest near Atlanta, Eddie's great
voice of command came booming out from under the
debris, only slightly muffled by the wreckage and the
dead man who lay on top of him. "Please be calm," he
ordered the rescuers. "Please don't light any matches."

It is the same in this story of his shipwreck. Inciden-
tally, no other raft story ever need be written because
it has everything—human skill and human error, the
tragedy of death and the unconquered struggle for life
—everything you can pack into twenty-one days and
three rubber rafts. Most of all it has Eddie Rickenbacker.
Because his great vigor emerges triumphant through the
literary spit and polish of the smooth sentences. Here
adrift on the Pacific is a powerful leader of men, battling
against the elements and against discouragement, fighting
despair with flaming bitterness, never relenting, never
compromising. And not always with tact, for there
was hardly time for that.

If this story lacks anything it is cannibalism and, had
it been longer, it might have had even that; for in another week I think his raft colleagues would, with relish,
have eaten Eddie. There is a limit to everything. Even
the tough old Pacific, after battling Eddie Rickenbacker
for twenty-one days, finally gave him up to the skies, I
would imagine with a weary sigh of relief along its
white beaches.

W. L. WHITE

# CHAPTER I

## Secret Orders

By way of preface I wish one point to be understood: what follows is almost all out of memory. I made no notes during our twenty-one days of drifting on the Pacific, and even if I had had paper for making them, the salt water and sweat which dissolved everything dissolvable would have left nothing but a pulp. Therefore, the sequence of events may be rather uncertain. What I may remember as happening on one day or another may, by my companions' recollections, have happened earlier or later. But such discrepancies, if they exist, are unimportant. My instinct then was not to remember but to live.

Again, men place different values on experiences shared together. What stirred or depressed me may have seemed inconsequential to the others. While I sit in a Rockefeller Plaza office which I have all to myself and where a push on a buzzer will summon nearly anything I need, much of what I went through on that ridiculously small raft now seems almost irrelevant. It is like trying to remember being dead.

The beginnings of this episode on the Pacific go back to March 1942. I was then in Miami, which is one of the headquarters of Eastern Air Lines. Lieutenant General Henry H. Arnold, Chief of the Army Air Forces and an old friend, called me from Washington and asked if I felt up to taking on a special job—a job he could discuss only in person. This was just about a year after the airplane crash at Atlanta, and while I was still lame, I could get around. I told General Arnold I'd be glad to do anything within my power.

I cleaned up my business in Miami over the week end and flew to Washington on a Sunday night. General Arnold's "special job" was an invitation to visit the various Army Air Force units being assembled in this country for overseas action. Naturally, I was glad to do it, and having planned an Easter holiday with my two boys in Miami, I told "Hap" I'd be ready to leave within two weeks.

"All right," he said, "but I'm sorry you can't make it earlier. A lot of the outfits will have left for overseas by then, and I'd like them to have the benefit of your knowledge of combat psychology from the last war."

With that I said I'd be ready to leave the following Monday.

General Arnold sent a ship with an Army crew down

to Miami on the appointed day, and to make a long story short I covered forty-three Air Force training stations, in practically every state, in thirty-two days. I visited all types of Air Force units—heavy, medium, and light bombardment, and fighter, and talked to from one to three groups every day.

The results were evidently useful enough to induce Secretary of War Stimson to offer me a world-wide mission to inspect United States air combat groups, both fighter and bomber, in all theaters of war. The assignment called for a report on the comparative values of United States aircraft and those of the enemy, together with my own opinions on air-fighting techniques. I was to be paid $1.00 a day, and at the request of Mr. Stimson I was appointed special consultant to him. This gave me the independence I wanted. In a way, I was the people's representative on American air power.

The first mission carried me to England, Ireland, and Iceland. I left in September and the trip was kept secret until I returned to Washington, early in October, to make my report.

I flew directly to England, where I spent fourteen days. In the course of the stay I met and talked with all the high commanding officers of the American fighter and bomber groups being assembled there. I went to the various airfields where they are based and asked questions of everyone—not only the officers, but the pilots and mechanics. Because part of the assignment was to compare American techniques with those employed by our Allies as well as our enemies, I also called upon all of the high commanding officers of the R.A.F. and most of the ranking British government officials concerned with air. It was one of the most interesting and instructive periods I have ever known.

When I had finished gathering my notes, I co-ordinated my information with that in the possession of our Ambassador, Mr. Winant, and Mr. Averell Harriman, our Lend-Lease representative in Britain. Ambassador Winant, I should explain, is no newcomer to the subject of air power. He flew in France during the last war and I first came to know him there.

The visit produced one wholly unexpected pleasure. At one of the airdromes outside London I met Prime Minister Churchill by chance. He was making one of his frequent inspections. He greeted me most cordially and after he had finished looking around, he invited me to ride back to London with him. On the way he asked if I would like to join him for lunch, and, of course, I was happy to accept.

This was my first visit to 10 Downing Street. The lunch was simple. The Canadian Minister of Munitions, Mr. Howe, whom I have known many years, and several other government officials were there. Mr. Churchill was in brilliant form. He discussed the general strategic situation, and because all of us had had a greater or lesser part in the last war, we talked about the changes in the

principles of fighting between this war and the other, and
the different kinds of weapons required. The talk carried
through the lunch hour, and over the coffee, and continued into the afternoon—at least three hours.

One statement that Mr. Churchill made stuck in my
mind. He was tremendously interested in bombers and
destroyers and several times he said:

"Give me another thousand heavy bombers and two
hundred more destroyers, and while I won't promise to
change the trend of the war, I will promise to shorten it."

Just a few days before a lone German raider had
crossed the Channel and dropped bombs on a boys'
school. The pilot had deliberately singled out the school
from all the military objectives upon which he might
have sighted his bombs. More than thirty boys were
killed, together with several instructors. I asked Mr.
Churchill why the British government had not used this
gruesome and inexcusable episode to whip up public
opinion against the enemy. Mr. Churchill answered:

"Naturally we are all heartbroken. It was unsporting
and cruel. But you must remember that we, too, are
bombing Germany every day. We are bombing her cities
and her people as hard as we can. The R.A.F. policy is
to bomb only military objectives, but the bombs do not
always hit them."

From England I returned by air via Ireland, Iceland,
and Canada, where I visited more United States air units.
I made my report to Mr. Stimson—a general paper which

was published, together with a memorandum on a long-range program which was confidential.

Five or six days later I headed into the Pacific. Here, as in the Atlantic area, my assignment was to visit the combat air bases, question the commanding officers, pilots, and ground crews, and make up my mind as to the good and bad. It was on this trip that I ran into trouble.

Accompanying me as aide, besides providing the necessary amount of gold braid to satisfy protocol, was an old friend—Colonel Hans Adamson. I have known him since he was aide to F. Trubee Davison, Assistant Secretary of War for Air in Hoover's Cabinet.

Adamson and I flew from New York to Los Angeles on the night of October 17, where I stopped only long enough to visit my mother, now in her eightieth year. Next evening I continued to San Francisco, and twenty-four hours later we met again aboard a Pan American Clipper, bound for Hawaii. It was a fine flight, putting us down in Honolulu on the morning of October 20, in the record time of fifteen hours.

My principal destinations were Australia, New Guinea, and Guadalcanal. I wanted to go on that same night. Lieutenant General Delos C. Emmons, commander of the Hawaiian Department, had been advised by Mr. Stimson of my coming. I talked with his staff and they showed me the Air Force units, and by evening I was ready to leave. Brigadier General William L. Lynd, commanding officer of Hickam Field, promised to have a ship ready by 10:30 P.M. I had hoped for a converted B-24 bomber, because it is roomier, but the only long-range four-engine plane available was a tactically obsolete Boeing Flying Fortress which had been earmarked for return to the United States for training uses.

I asked General Lynd about the crew. He assured me they were experienced men, all members of the Army Air Transport Command, several with air line experience.

That night General Lynd drove Colonel Adamson and myself to Hickam Field. Our bags went into the cabin, followed by a dozen sacks of high-priority mail for the different headquarters en route. I was told there would be an extra passenger—Sergeant Alexander Kaczmarczyk, a ground-crew chief. He had been taken off a transport because he had yellow jaundice, and while recovering from this had come down with appendicitis. Now he was en route to Australia to rejoin his unit.

We got going. The plane was making 80 m.p.h. on the flat when I felt it lunge to the left, and saw the dark shadows of the hangars rushing up. The thought crossed my mind: "Hickam gets another blitz and Rickenbacker's part of it." The pilot, by clever manipulation of the engines, managed to swing back onto the runway. By the time he reached the end of the field, the speed had worn off enough for him to risk a violent ground loop, which saved us from plunging into the bay.

A broken hydraulic line on the starboard brake system

was at fault. Captain Cherry, the pilot, was too young to walk when I commanded the pursuit squadron on the Western Front. But he was happy-go-lucky, like so many Texans are. He brushed off the accident, saying: "We got more of these, Captain. The crew and I will stand by until another plane is ready." I thought: "Well, it had better not be like the first."

General Lynd drove me back to his quarters and shortly after midnight word came that another ship, also a Flying Fortress, was ready. The baggage and mail were already aboard and General Lynd had thoughtfully added a cot for Adamson and myself. I asked Captain Cherry about the weather ahead. High, scattered clouds, he answered, but clear—"an uneventful flight," was the forecast.

And so it was—through the first nine hours. Off at 1:30 A.M., October 21, we squared away on the course for Island X, 1,800 miles or so to the southwest. The night was beautiful—high, thin clouds, a three-quarter moon. I sat for an hour in the cockpit, enjoying the night and the small talk, then walked aft to the tail for a few hours' sleep, Colonel Adamson joining me. By then we were at 10,000 feet and although I had a blanket around me, and a trench coat, I was cold and slept only in snatches.

At 6:30 daylight broke. I had orange juice and coffee from the thermos jugs, and a sweet roll. Forward in the cockpit everything seemed serene. Captain Cherry said we were due to make our landfall at 9:30 A.M.

An hour before that time Cherry started downhill, gliding from 9,000 to 1,000 feet. That was when we started to look for our island. We kept on looking and I, for one, have yet to see it.

The sun climbed high in the port quarter, and while the clouds were heavier, huge stretches of blue sky showed between. At 10:15 A.M., three quarters of an hour beyond the expected arrival time, Captain Cherry was still holding to the original course. I asked how much gas he had. "A little over four hours," he said. I was sitting directly behind him. In fact, I was glued there, because a wholly unreasonable premonition that we were in trouble had lodged in my mind. In a little while I asked how much tail wind we were supposed to have. The answer was about ten miles.

Call it hindsight, if you want, since I certainly had no way of telling, but I was sure we had been flying faster than we knew. Inside me the feeling grew that we had overshot the mark and were moving away from it, into the open Pacific. One daybreak weeks later, in the cockpit of another bomber bound for Brisbane, Australia, I was to learn how it happened. The officer beside me then mentioned casually that he had been navigator on an airplane that had left Hickam Field, bound for the same Island X, just an hour before we did. He, too, had been given the same tail-wind forecast, but a check on his speed had convinced him it was three times as strong and he had corrected accordingly.

It was our bad luck not to be aware of this. At the speed we were making, the airplane must have been beyond Island X before Captain Cherry started downhill. All this time the radio operator was in routine contact with Island X, and the navigator, in the astro-hatch, was trying to shoot the sun. About ten-thirty I suggested to the pilot that he ask Island X for bearings. Island X replied it couldn't give us a bearing—it had no equipment. So we tried Island Y, another United States outpost, some distance east and north of the first. Island Y instructed us to climb to 5,000 feet and circle for thirty minutes, sending out a radio signal, while they took a bearing. This we did. They supplied us with a compass course, which meant nothing; we could be on it, yet a thousand miles below or above the island. Nevertheless, we let down through the cloud layer and lined up on the new course which took us west. We flew on, at better than three miles a minute, but all we saw was water and more water.

It was plain now that we were lost, and the first slight signs of nervousness appeared in the crew. The young navigator, after half-a-dozen first-class Pacific crossings, was baffled by his failure. Then the only possible explanation occurred to him: his octant, which had been on the navigation table, must have been badly jarred when the first airplane ground-looped at Hickam Field. This alone could have thrown his observations off—perhaps by several degrees. So it is probable that the positions subsequently obtained were erroneous. It is easy, then, to understand how we could have passed the island far to the left or right.

I present these facts not in criticism but in explanation. Whoever travels in wartime must expect risks. Weather and radio aids that are commonplace in commercial airline operations do not yet exist in the Pacific; nor is there always time for thorough inspection. If the Army had waited for prissy safeguards there would be no American air power in the Pacific today.

There was nothing to do but fall back on the last resort of the lost and box the compass. I shall not dwell on the next few hours. We turned every which way. We even asked Island X to fire their anti-aircraft guns, setting the shells to burst at 7,000 feet, well above the cloud level. We also asked them to send out planes, on the chance they might see us, or we them. Both were done, but although we rose to 8,000 feet and circled we saw nothing.

In due time, like all others lost on the Pacific, we got what airmen call "island eyes." You see land because you want to see it and have to see it, and with all of us at the windows, every cloud shadow momentarily held the promise of land.

Captain Cherry, coming down low over the sea, leaned the mixture, but our time and gasoline were running out. The radio operator kept calling for bearings, hoping that someone would be able to take a cross bearing on us. At

1:30 P.M. Captain Cherry turned east, doubling back on his tracks. The clouds were thinning out and he climbed back to 5,000 feet to see better, and to save gasoline he cut out the two outboard engines. The only hope now was to find a ship. After talking to Captain Cherry I wrote out a radio message saying one hour's fuel remained —the last message heard by anyone. The operator started to pound out S O S's and he did not stop until a second or two before the plane hit. No one heard it.

The fact that the S O S went unacknowledged meant that in addition to our not knowing where we were, none of the islands from which a search might be started knew, either. And that, I remarked to Adamson, was a hell of a fine place to start from or be looked for.

Realizing what we were in for, I found myself studying my companions. Other than Adamson, they were strangers. Adamson was three months older than I, and I had had my fifty-second birthday in Scotland a few weeks before. In his youth Hans had been an explorer, but like me he had become a desk man and paper shuffler. Too old to fight but familiar with war, he and I were not expected to face hardships or risks; these were for younger men.

In the moments before the crash Hans, too, must have been thinking hard, because he said with a grim smile, "Rick, I hope you like the sea. I think we're going to spend a long time on it."

As for the crew, the oldest man was the copilot, Lieutenant Whittaker, a heavy-set, self-assured fellow of about forty. All that I knew about him came from a few remarks he had dropped—that he had been a contractor and promoter in civilian life, and before joining the Air Force had done most of his flying in private airplanes. The navigator, Lieutenant De Angelis, was only twenty-three; he was a short, wiry, thoughtful kid, with black curly hair. Private Bartek, the flight engineer, was the same age. Sergeant Reynolds, the radioman, was a tall, skinny chap, several years older, with an air of quiet competence.

Then there was the extra man—Sergeant Alex. He had had little to say, and, studying him, I thought he looked frail. As for Captain Cherry, I knew nothing about him either, except that he had been a copilot on American Airlines. Only twenty-seven, he had the gay and buoyant disposition of most airmen. In the cynical way of an older man who had had his share of trouble, I thought, "Well, my young friend, your cowboy boots and goatee are going to look pretty damn funny in the middle of the Pacific."

The last minutes ran out fast. The instant Cherry wheeled east all of us accepted the inevitability of a crash landing. We made ready to throw overboard everything that was movable. I helped Sergeant Alex pry open the bottom hatch in the tail and between us we dumped all that high-priority mail into the blue Pacific. Then the toolbox, the cots, the blankets, the empty thermos bottles, a brand-new Burberry coat I had bought only a few weeks before in London, and all the baggage, including a beautiful suitcase that the boys and girls of Eastern Air Lines had given me for Christmas two years before. I had frugally removed a spare bridge that my dentist had just made for me, but after a second's deliberation I threw that away too. After it went my brief case, bulging with papers of which no copies existed—papers that I had considered important. Let the moment come when nothing is left but life and you will find that you do not hesitate over the fate of material possessions, however deeply they may have been cherished.

We made all possible preparations for the crash. The remaining thermos bottles were filled with water and coffee. With the emergency rations, which were stowed in a small metal box, they were piled on the deck in the radio compartment, just below the hatch from which we planned to leave. Sergeant Alex dumped half a can of condensed milk into a thermos jug, saying, "I've got to have cream in my coffee." Poor Alex, he had already had his last coffee and cream that morning. Adamson suggested maybe we'd better drink our fill of water, but I advised against it, thinking we might need it more later on. As Adamson was later to remind me, that was probably the worst advice he had ever been given.

Before dumping the suitcase, I had snatched out a handful of handkerchiefs, including three handsome ones —a blue, a gray, and a brown—that Mrs. Rickenbacker

had bought for me some years ago in Paris. I had a hunch
then they might be useful in protecting us from the sun.
I also broke open a couple of cartons of cigarettes, passing the packages around, keeping two or three for myself. Adamson, Sergeant Alex, and De Angelis had meanwhile propped the mattresses against the bulkheads, to
cushion the shock if we were thrown forward. All of us,
by then, had put on Mae West life jackets.

Lean as the mixture was, the two engines ran sweetly,
but our ears were listening for the first dry splutter.
There were eight of us, and if the plane survived the
crash, we could count on three life rafts. Two were so-
called five-man rafts in compartments on opposite sides
of the plane, which Bartek was to expel by pulling levers
in the cockpit. There was also a two-man raft rolled up
in the radio compartment. This was placed with the little
pile of seagoing rations.

We had worked out a plan for abandoning ship, even
to the point of assigning stations on the rafts. The Fortress is, of course, a land plane, weighing about twenty-
five tons. Many have been force-landed at sea in this war,
and while a few had stayed afloat longer, Cherry could
not safely count on more than thirty to sixty seconds.
So we'd have to be quick. Unwilling to burden myself,
yet fearful of leaving something indispensable behind, I
rummaged through my remaining possessions. I stuffed
the map inside my shirt; my passport and the official
papers that Mr. Stimson had given me I stowed in an

inside pocket. A frugal instinct caused me to pocket a chocolate bar and to salvage a sixty-foot length of line, which I wound around my body. The last thing I did before sitting down was to help Sergeant Alex loosen the hatch, lest it be jammed in the crash.

Somebody brought back word that Cherry was starting down. The plane dipped into a long glide. Adamson was sitting on the deck, his back braced against one of the mattresses. De Angelis was lying on the floor, pressed against the other. Sergeant Reynolds was at his little desk, watching the busy dials on the panel, while his fingers played out the S O S that no one ever heard. Squatting behind him was Sergeant Alex. I was on the right-hand side, strapped in the seat, holding a parachute to protect my face. From the window I could see the ocean coming closer. For the first time I realized that it was quite rough, with a long, heavy swell.

The others kept asking "How much longer?" and I kept answering "Not yet, not yet." The pilots, Cherry and Whittaker, were, of course, forward, and Bartek was standing behind the latter, with his hands on the levers for springing the big rafts. Somebody across from me said, "Only fifty feet left." And an instant later one engine sputtered, choked, and died. "Hold on!" I shouted. "Here it comes!" Reynolds bent his head, but he did not take his hand off the key.

The crash was a violent jumble of sounds and motions. Only once before had I ever heard such sounds: that was when I crashed at Atlanta. Pieces of the radio equipment bolted to the bulkhead flew about like shrapnel. A fraction of a second later, while we were still stunned from the first crash, a second one came and with that the plane lost motion. I doubt if from where the belly first grazed the water to where we stopped dead was more than fifty feet. As I struggled to unfasten myself, green water was pouring over my legs and down my back. The window beside me had been broken and the topside hatch had carried away. The whole Pacific Ocean seemed to be rushing in.

But it was a wonderful landing, timed to the second. Young Cherry laid his airplane down in the middle of a trough, and killed her off against the waning slope of a swell. Had he miscalculated by two seconds and hit the crest, I would not be telling this now. The Fortress would have gone straight on to the bottom of the sea.

Adamson staggered to his feet, moaning about his back. Sergeant Alex and De Angelis looked all right, but Sergeant Reynolds had his hands to his face and blood was running through his fingers. He had been jerked against the radio panel. When he took his hands away I saw a bloody, gaping slash across his nose. I heard Bartek yell that the rafts were free. Then the two pilots splashed aft to give us a hand.

All of us were badly shaken up, and it seemed to take forever for us to clear out. Adamson and I being supercargo, the crew insisted we go first. I stood on the arm of the seat and hauled myself through the hatch, while the others shoved from below. Once on the wing I was able to give them a hand. Bartek, who had escaped through the forward hatch, was already on the wing, which was barely awash. The two rafts, which had automatically inflated themselves when expelled, were buoyant on the swell, one on each side of the plane. But the line holding mine had become fouled, and in trying to free it, Bartek had cut his fingers to the bone. Blood reddened everything he touched.

"So this," I thought, "is the placid Pacific." The swells were twice as high as I am tall, which is tall enough, and with the submerged plane surging and heaving from crest to trough, it was hard to keep a footing. With Bartek's help, I managed to free my raft and work it alongside the wing so that Adamson, who was in great pain from his hurt back, could slide down. It was difficult getting into the raft in that heavy swell, but in such circumstances the difficult things of life become normal and the impossible ones take a little longer. After Adamson got in, Bartek slid down the wing and crawled into the raft, while I held the line. When I tried to coil my one-hundred-and-eighty-five-pound frame in the stern, there wasn't enough room left for a midget.

Cherry, Whittaker, and Sergeant Reynolds were already clear in the other big raft; but the two-man affair was upside down, and Alex and De Angelis were splashing wildly in the water, trying to push it back to the wing. It had tipped over when Alex stepped in, throwing both him and the other man overboard. They managed to right it and get aboard. By that time I was in difficulty. Before I could break out the two little aluminum oars secured to the inside of my raft, a swell had washed us against the tail of the Fortress and we just missed being overturned. As it was, the raft filled with water.

I really don't know how long it took us to do all these things, but we were quicker than we thought. Although deep down, the Fortress was still afloat. A good deal of shouting was going on between the rafts, and after we had drifted fifty yards or so downwind, somebody called out: "Who has the water?"

No one had it. No one had the rations, either.

I am quite sure that none of us wholly understood, then, what this meant. Life by itself seemed the most adequate of rations. If it seems odd that we should have left the food and water after all the careful preparations, I can only say that the shock and confusion, the hurt men, the rough seas, the trouble with the rafts, drove the thought of them out of mind. By the time the last man got out, the water was feet deep inside the plane; the pile of things we had collected was somewhere underneath, scattered by the crash. After arguing back and forth, we decided not to re-enter the plane, lest somebody get caught inside when it sank. This was another mistake. The Fortress stayed afloat nearly six minutes. I was bailing with my hat when I heard a shout: "There she goes!" The tail swung upright, in true ship's fashion, hesitated, then slid quickly out of sight.

By my watch it was 2:36 P.M. on the afternoon of October 21.

# CHAPTER II

# The Death of Sergeant Alex

THE LINE AROUND MY WAIST was now put to good use. Because the wind and seas were fast sweeping the rafts apart, I called the others in and, fastening the rope to the hand lines around the rafts, we formed a line astern, twenty feet or so apart. Cherry being captain, his raft was first, mine was second, and the two-man raft brought up the rear. The arrangement had its drawbacks. In the heavy swell, as the rafts rose and fell at their different intervals, the interminable, uneven shocks on the line made rest impossible. But I shall always believe that had we separated, few if any of us would now be alive. A strong man may last a long time alone but men together somehow manage to last longer.

My memory of that first afternoon is not wholly clear. The spray and the green water coming over the roll of the raft kept us soaked, and I bailed for hours with my hat—my wonderful old hat. This gave me exercise, besides keeping me from thinking too much.

Some time during the afternoon we totted up our possessions. The only food was four oranges that Cherry had stuffed in his pocket just before the crash, together with the chocolate bar that I had and half a dozen more that Alex had, which an Army doctor had given him the day before. The chocolate was never eaten. Alex' was ruined by his thrashing around in the water and he had to throw it away. Next day, when I felt in the pocket for mine, it had become a green mush, which neither I nor my companions would touch.

So, except for the oranges, we started with nothing. But knowing that a man can live a long time without food or water, I was more worried over the shortage of clothing. Only Adamson and I were fully dressed. He had his uniform and cap and I had on a blue summer-weight business suit, complete with necktie, pocket handkerchief, and refillable pencil. The others, expecting to swim, had taken off their shoes and hats before abandoning ship. None had hats or sweaters, but the two pilots had their leather jackets. Several had even thrown their socks away. Bartek, in fact, was naked except for a one-piece jumper.

I may have forgotten an item or two, but these were our total possessions: a first-aid kit, eighteen flares, and one Very pistol for firing them; two hand pumps for both bailing and renewing the air in the rafts; two service sheath knives; a pair of pliers; a small pocket compass; two revolvers belonging to Cherry and Adamson; two collapsible rubber bailing buckets; three sets of patching gear, one for each raft; several pencils; and my map of the Pacific. We all had cigarettes, but the salt water got to these immediately, and they were thrown away. And, finally, Reynolds produced two fish lines, with hooks attached, which he had snatched from a parachute bag after the crash. But there was no bait, and unless we managed to shoot down a gull, our chances of "living off the country" were decidedly thin.

But that first afternoon no one was conscious of our poverty; we were too exhausted to care. Three or four of the boys were violently seasick and I didn't feel any too comfortable myself, although I never reached the point of vomiting. Adamson was in agony from his wrenched back; every jerk of the boat, he said, felt as if someone was kicking him in the kidneys. But I was more worried about Sergeant Alex, in the little raft astern. Long after the others had stopped, he continued to retch. "What's the matter with him?" I called to De Angelis. "I don't know," answered De Angelis, "he must have swallowed a lot of salt water when we tipped over."

The sun went down swiftly, a cold mist gathering on the sea, and the moon came up—a three-quarter moon—beautiful to see. The wisecracks and the small talk, which sounded pretty silly in the immensity of the night, petered out and we were beginning to realize that we were in for hard times.

Naturally, one of the first things we had to do was to

work out some organization of habits. Keeping a continuous watch—what we called an alert—was an obvious necessity. That first night we arranged to stand two-hour watches, relieving each other in turn. It seems pretty silly now, but I offered $100 to the first man to see land, a ship, or an airplane. But nobody slept that night. We were wet and miserable. Although the swell moderated just before midnight, the waves kept slopping into the rafts. Both air and water were warm, yet with each splash I felt as if I was being doused with buckets of ice water. Bartek and I changed positions every hour or so, to share the comfort of the other's lee. But I was never warm, and put in most of the night bailing. Sharks followed us from the plane; the water seemed full of them.

The second day came on slowly, first a gray mist and then the sun breaking through clear. It took hours to get warm, for the night mist penetrated to the bone. As I have said, we had those four oranges, but we decided to save them against the future. By popular vote I was made their custodian, and Cherry generously handed them over. We agreed to divide the first that morning, and the others on alternate days. That way, they would last eight days.

I cut the orange in half, then halved the halves, then halved the quarters, giving each man one eighth. With seven men watching, you can be sure I made an exact division. In fact, I studied the fruit a full minute before I cut. Some sucked and ate the peel, but Cherry and I saved ours for bait.

Men have been lost at sea before; others have spent more days on rafts than we did. A good deal of what we went through was what you might expect—hunger, thirst, heat, cold, and a slow rotting away. In some respects, the period from the second to the eighth day was the worst. A glassy calm fell upon the sea; the sun beat down fiercely all day; the rafts stood still, with the lines slack between; I even imagined I smelled flesh burning, and the sweet stink of hot rubber.

Face, neck, hands, wrists, legs, and ankles burned, blistered, turned raw, and burned again. In time De Angelis and Whittaker, having darker skins, developed a protecting tan, but the rest of us cooked day after day. My hands swelled and blistered; when the salt water got into the flesh, it burned and cracked and dried and burned again. Three months later the scars still show on the knuckles. Our mouths became covered with ugly running sores. Reynolds, having no covering for his legs, turned into a sodden red mass of hurt. Even the soles of his feet were burned raw.

These first five or six days were the worst I have ever known. The night I lay in a wrecked plane near Atlanta, with a dead man half crushed under my chest, had produced its own kind of suffering. But then the pain had been dulled by delirium, and after a while I knew help was near because I could hear people moving around in the dark. But on the Pacific I was something being turned on a spit. Without my hat, I would have been badly off.

I would fill it with water, then jam it down over my ears. Before our rescue, the brim was half torn away from the crown.

Some of the others, to escape the terrible heat, paddled for hours in the water. But they paid a stiff price for the relief because their flesh burned again as it dried, and the salt brine stung. Without my handkerchiefs we would have had a much harder time. I passed them around and, folded bandit-fashion across the nose, they protected the lower part of the face. But there was no sparing the eyes. The sea sent back billions of sharp splinters of light; no matter where one looked it was painful. A stupor descended upon the rafts. Men simply sat or sprawled, heads rolling on the chest, mouths half open, gasping. Reynolds, from the cut on his nose, was a horrible sight. The sun would not let the wound heal. He washed the blood off with salt water, but it soon oozed again, spreading over his face, drying in a red crust. Bartek, too, was in agony from his cut fingers. He splashed them with iodine from the first-aid kit, but the salt water ate it away.

Daytimes we prayed for the coolness of the nights; nights we craved the sun. But I really came to hate the nights. Daytimes, I could see my fellow men, the play of the water, the gulls, all the signs of life. But the night brought us all close to fear. A cold, dense mist always rose around us. The damp soaked our clothes and we pressed together for warmth. Sometimes, when the mist was very heavy, the other rafts would be hidden. If the sea was calm and the line had fallen slack, I would sometimes come out of a nightmare, and pull in the towlines until they fetched up hard, and I knew the others were still there. Other times, I would hear moans or groans, or a cry and often a prayer. Or I would see a shadow move and twist as a man tried to ease his torture.

I know I can never hope to describe the awful loneliness of the night. Perhaps it affected me more than the others. I seldom slept more than an hour or so at a time, and even then, it seemed, with one eye open and one ear cocked. That was because I was always worried that the man who was supposed to be on watch might doze off and let a ship go by. I have gotten along most of my life with a good deal less sleep than most men are accustomed to have. This habit stood me in good stead on the Pacific. But the younger men had trouble staying awake. The stupor induced by the terrific heat of the day, together with the lulling motion of the raft as it listed and fell on the swell—a motion that at times was not unlike that of a hammock—seemed to put them quickly to sleep.

What also made the night hard for me was that I could never stretch out. Someday I shall meet the man who decided these rafts could hold two men and five men each. When I do, he is either going to revise his opinions or prove them on a long voyage, under conditions I shall be happy to suggest. Adamson weighed over two hundred pounds and I was not much lighter. On our five-man raft, he and Bartek and I shared an inside room measuring six feet nine inches by two feet four inches. Counting the narrow inflated roll, on which a man could stretch out for an hour or so with his feet dangling in the water, the dimensions were nine feet by five.

Because Adamson was in such pain, Bartek and I gave him one end to himself. He lay with his bumpus on the bottom, his head against the carbon-dioxide bottle, his feet across the roll. Bartek and I lay facing each other, or back to back, with our legs crooked over the roll. This was the way it was in Cherry's boat. But Alex and De Angelis in the two-man raft, although the smallest men, were much worse off. They had to sit facing each other, one with his legs over the other man's shoulders, while he took the legs of the other under his armpits, or they sat back to back, dangling their legs in the water. And sometimes De Angelis lay sprawled out, with Alex on his chest. Imagine two men in a small, shallow bathtub, and you will have a reasonably good idea of how much room they had.

Whenever you turned or twisted, you forced the others to turn or twist. It took days to learn how to make the most of the space, at an incalculable price in misery. A foot or hand or shoulder, moved in sleep or restlessness, was bound to rake the raw flesh of a companion. With the flesh, tempers turned raw and many things said in the night had best be forgotten.

The moon was turning into full. I was awake a good

part of the time, hoping to catch the loom of a ship. In those first nights of utter calm the clouds would form the most unusual pictures, beautiful women, elephants, birds. It sounds fantastic. I remember seeing one shaped like a wild boar. I saw trees, completely formed.

The first two or three nights I thought I was seeing things. Finally I mentioned it to Adamson and he agreed with me that they were there. There was some reason for them because you could see them night in and night out, particularly during the first ten days. The moonlight helped to make these forms seem more vivid. I suppose there is a scientific explanation but I don't know what it is.

The forms were so vivid, so concise, so positive that they fascinated me. This helped some; it gave me something to think about during the long hours of the night.

The stars helped also to keep our minds occupied. We were on the equator and so all the familiar stars were in different positions, the Big Dipper, the Little Dipper, the North Star. We used to talk about them. Colonel Adamson had been in charge of the Planetarium in New York for a number of years and he was able to tell us a great deal about the different constellations and the movements of the stars. I kept promoting these discussions because of the good it did all of us.

What bothered us most of all was not knowing where we were. Every member of the party had his own ideas about this. I was under the impression—and later events confirmed it—that we were somewhere west or northwest of our island destination. Captain Cherry agreed with me in this.

The next day a terrible calm settled down which made the sea just like a glassy mirror. There were very little swells only and the sun was intensely hot. The glare was terrible on the eyes and most of the boys fell into a doze or sort of stupor. Most of them had injuries of one kind or another to add to their plight. I was afraid that Sergeant Reynolds had a broken nose. In getting out he had struck his head against the radio and the blood had dried on his face. He had no hat and the sun was beginning to burn him badly, and the combination made him an awesome-looking spectacle. Bartek had had all his fingers cut on the inside of the hand, two of them to the bone, and they had bled very badly. We had hauled out the iodine from the first-aid kit as soon as we settled down on the rafts and had done what we could to dress the fingers. The effect did not last long because the salt water would take it off. It would get into the little cuts and so kept him in agony for the first two or three nights. Finally, of course, it dried out and started to heal.

On the fourth morning the second orange was divided. Except for the orange on the second morning, we had then been seventy-two hours without food or liquid. Fish were all around; I could see hundreds swimming idly just below the raft. Cherry and I fished for hours with pieces of orange peel. I even borrowed Adamson's keyring,

which was shiny, and tried to manipulate it as a spinner.
The fish would nose the hook, fan their tails in curiosity,
but they never struck.

For six days on that glassy, sizzling sea, the rafts did
not seem to move. But by our watches we knew we were
drifting; each morning the sun rose just a little bit later.
This meant the rafts were inching west and south. We
argued interminably over where we were, but it turned
out only Cherry and I were right. We were positive of
having overshot our island and, if our guess was true, we
could count on no land nearer than certain Japanese-held
islands four hundred to five hundred miles away. I
studied the map two or three times a day, always returning it to my inside coat pocket, to protect it against the
water. But the colors were already beginning to run.

Commencing the second night, Cherry sent up a flare
every night. Having eighteen, we first decided to use
three a night, the first after sundown, the second around
midnight, the last before dawn. But of the first three sent
aloft, one was a complete dud and the second flickered
for only a few seconds. The third, swinging on its parachute, gave a scary, blinding red light, lasting perhaps a
minute and a half. Next night, cutting down the expendi-
ture to two good ones, we had another dud; this decided
us to reduce the nightly allotment to a single good one.

Always, after the light had exhausted itself, my eyes
strained into the darkness, hoping to catch a responding
gleam—a gleam which would not settle into the steadiness

of a star. It was plain that unless we soon had food or water or the terrible hot calm relented, some of us were bound to die. Adamson, being portly, felt the heat worse than the rest. Reynolds, thin anyway, was fading to skin and bones. Alex, though, was really in a bad way. His mouth was dry and frothing; he cried continually for water. He was only a boy—barely twenty-two—and thinking he was quitting, I pulled his raft in close and asked why the hell he couldn't take it? It was a brutal thing to do, yet I was determined to shock him back to his senses. I found out then what was wrong. He was only three weeks out of the hospital. In addition, he had contracted a lip disease, something like trench mouth, with a scientific name I do not remember. All this had left him with less strength than the rest from the start, and the salt water he swallowed when his raft capsized had helped to do him in.

Unfortunately for him that wasn't the only salt water Alex had had. De Angelis woke one night to find him half out of the raft, gulping salt water. Now I had admonished everybody the first afternoon out not to drink salt water, knowing that it would drive them wild with thirst. Alex admitted he had been doing this persistently. It explained the cries for water we didn't have. "I tried not to," Alex said, "but I had to. I just had to have water."

So it was only a question of time for poor Alex. He

sank deeper into delirium, murmuring his "Hail Mary" and other Catholic prayers. In his wallet was a photograph of a young girl to whom he was engaged: he talked to it, prayed over it. Finally he could neither sleep nor lie down. De Angelis tried to keep the sun off him, but there was no shadow anywhere. So he burned and burned. At night in the moonlight I could see him sitting on the raft shaking as if with ague. He literally vibrated, he was so horribly cold. Yet, except to cry for water, he never really complained.

Bartek had a New Testament in his jumper pocket. Watching him read it, the thought came to me that we might all profit by his example. I am not a religious man, but I was taught the Lord's Prayer at my mother's knee and I had gone to Sunday school. If I had any religion in my later life, it was based on the Golden Rule. Yet I have always been conscious of God.

With the New Testament as an inspiration, we held morning and evening prayers. The rafts were pulled together, making a rough triangle. Then, each in turn, one of us would read a passage. None of us, I must confess, showed himself to be very familiar with them, but thumbing the book we found a number that one way or another bespoke our needs. The Twenty-third Psalm was, of course, a favorite. I have always been stirred by it, but out on the Pacific I found a beauty in it that I had never appreciated. Yet there was another that we never failed to read, because it so clearly set forth what was in our minds:

*Therefore take no thought, saying, What shall we eat? or, What shall we drink? or, Wherewithal shall we be clothed?*

*. . . For your heavenly Father knoweth that ye have need of all these things. But seek ye first the kingdom of God, and his righteousness; and all these things shall be added unto you.*

*Take therefore no thought for the morrow: for the morrow shall take thought for the things of itself. Sufficient unto the day is the evil thereof.* (Matthew 6:31–34.)

One or two turned scornful and bitter because the answer was slow in coming, but the rest went on praying with deep-felt hope. Yet we did not neglect anything that might help us to help ourselves. Whittaker tried to make a spear from one of the aluminum oars, tearing the flat corners away with the pliers. He drove it into the back of a shark which rubbed alongside, but the hide was tougher than the point. After several tries it was so blunted as to be useless. Whittaker threw it angrily into the bottom of the raft. He had gained nothing and wasted an oar.

Also, Cherry sat all day long with a loaded revolver in his lap, hoping to knock down a gull. But none came close enough for a shot. He broke the revolver open two or three times a day and rubbed the moving parts with oil from his nose and the back of his ears, but he could not halt the sea-water corrosion. When the parts froze solid he threw the gun into the Pacific. Adamson's gun rusted in the same way and I dropped it over the side.

To keep the sick men alive, we finished the oranges faster than we had intended. We had the third on the morning of the fifth day, the last on the sixth. The last two were shrunken, much of the juice appeared to have evaporated, and the last one was beginning to rot. So long as there was that sliver of orange to anticipate, no one complained of hunger. Now, memories of food and drink began to haunt us. We tried to catch the sharks that cruised near the rafts with our hands. I actually had several small ones by the back but the hide was too slippery for a firm grip.

The desire for food in several men became almost violent. They agonized over their hunger pains and talked constantly about food, and whether they could go on much longer without it.

Reynolds talked about how much soda pop he was going to drink the rest of his life. Cherry couldn't think about anything but chocolate ice cream. As I listened to the thirsty talk between the rafts, my own mind slowly filled with visions of chocolate malted milk. I could actually taste it, to the point where my tongue worked convulsively. The strange part is that I hadn't had a chocolate malted milk in nearly twenty-five years.

From the start I had advised against talk as I realized

how necessary it was going to be for all of us to conserve our strength in every way possible; but looking
back now I am rather amazed at the little talking that we
did.

During the first few days, while we suffered from the
shock of the fall and our minds were filled with specula-
tion as to the chances of rescue, there was much more
than later. This was particularly noticeable after several
days had passed and the prospect of escape was becoming dimmer. It was then we began to sing hymns after
prayer meetings. The singing seemed to release something in the minds of most of us and the talk for the first
time became intensely personal. As I have already stated,
there was no time that I lost faith in our ultimate rescue,
but the others did not seem to share this state of mind
fully with me. My companions clearly began to think of
what lay beyond death and to think of it in terms of their
own lives.

They began to tell of what they had experienced in
life: their hopes, fears, ambitions, their achievements,
their mistakes. I suppose it takes the imminence of death
to release one completely from inhibitions. The talk was
entirely honest and, I am sure, entirely frank. What was
said will always be locked up in our minds. As far as I
am concerned, no hint of those long, man-to-man con-
versations will ever be revealed. I am sure of one thing,
that it did us a great deal of good.

As the days wore on and our strength left us, we

talked less and less. A drowsiness, which in the later stages amounted almost to coma, had taken possession of us. We would lie for hours in the intense heat of the sun without a single word being spoken. What I seem to remember most about the last days was the almost complete silence. If one man spoke there would be no response. We were so completely divorced from living that we had nothing to talk about, even if we had had the strength for it.

I recall no mention of the war. It was continually in my own mind because of my conviction of survival. I was sure I would live to see the struggle through, and consequently did not get away from the speculations that I would have engaged in under normal conditions. I never put them into words, however. If my companions were thinking along the same line, they observed the same reticence that I did.

All conversation during the last stages had to do with the changes of position we found necessary in the rafts and the negative results of the Very lights we set off. Sometimes our hopes would kindle when one of us mistook a low star for the light of a ship. There would be eager discussion then, dwindling off into hopeless silences when it became certain that it had been nothing more than a delusion.

Twenty-one days of it, and during all that time, I am inclined to believe, we talked less than we would have done in the course of one normal day.

The eighth day was another hot, flat calm. It did not help our stomachs any to look down and see dolphin and mackerel, sleek and fat and twelve to eighteen inches long, and thousands of smaller fish swimming in the depths. That afternoon Cherry read the service, with the usual quotation from Matthew. About an hour later, when I was dozing with my hat pulled down over my eyes, a gull appeared from nowhere and landed on my hat.

I don't remember how it happened or how I knew he was there. But I knew it instantly, and I knew that if I missed this one, I'd never find another to sit on my hat. I reached up for him with my right hand—gradually. The whole Pacific seemed to be shaking from the agitation in my body, but I could tell he was still there from the hungry, famished, almost insane eyes in the other rafts. Slowly and surely my hand got up there; I didn't clutch, but just closed my fingers, sensing his nearness, then closing my fingers hard.

I wrung his neck, defeathered him, carved up the body, divided the meat into equal shares, holding back only the intestines for bait. Even the bones were chewed and swallowed. No one hesitated because the meat was raw and stringy and fishy. It tasted fine. After Cherry had finished his piece, I baited a hook and passed it over to him. The hook, weighted with Whittaker's ring, had hardly got wet before a small mackerel hit it, and was jerked into the raft. I dropped the other line, with the same miraculous result, except that mine was a small sea bass.

All this food in the space of a few minutes bolstered us beyond words. We ate one of the fish before dark and put the other aside for the next day. Even the craving for water seemed to abate, perhaps from chewing the cool, wet flesh while grinding the bones to a pulp. Alex and Adamson ate their shares, and I was optimistic enough to believe they were immediately better. I say in all truth that at no time did I ever doubt we would be saved, but as that eighth night rose around us I was sure we could last forever. The ocean was full of fish, and we could catch them.

As the sun went down, the sky clouded over, the air turned cool, a soft, uncertain wind made cat's-paws on the water—all portents of rain. I tried to stay awake to have everything in readiness if it came, but I finally dozed off with my head across Adamson's knees.

My next recollection is of being jolted awake, as if from a blow. The raft was slamming up and down on a heavy, irregular swell. It was pitch black—so black that I could scarcely make out the other rafts, except when they were thrown up on a swell. Gusts of wind came at us from every quarter. And I knew, if I ever knew anything, that rain was near.

From midnight we were on the watch for the rushing shadows of rain squalls. About three o'clock in the morning I heard the cry, "Rain." Drops splattered against my face and mouth, clean and sweet to taste. After the first few drops there was nothing more, but far off I could see the squall. The wind had a new sound, as if it were no longer empty. We paddled toward the squall and I prayed to God to put us in its path. We had a plan all worked out—bailing buckets ready and the empty canvas covers for the Very light cartridges. We took our shirts and socks off to spread over our heads and shoulders. The handkerchiefs were to be laid on the inflated roll until they became soaked. Adamson had even taken off his shorts to wring.

It was one hell of a night—all wind, waves, noise, lightning, and big black shadows. We paddled into it, shouting at the tops of our lungs. Out of that uproar came a cry for help. The little raft, with De Angelis and Alex, had broken loose. Bartek and I, with an oar to the side, set out after them, Cherry's raft following in our wake. I was afraid we'd lost them, but we sighted the raft against the white rush of a breaking wave, overtook it, and made it fast. A moment later the squall enveloped us.

Rain fell as from a waterfall. I spread the handkerchiefs on the roll of the raft, where they would catch the water, and fluffed my shirt over my head. Adamson, roused by the cool water on his body, draped his underpants over his chest to catch more water. I appointed myself wringer, and as fast as the others passed over the soaked pieces of cloth, I would twist them hard, forcing the water out, to rid the cloth of salt rime. I had done this several times with each piece, always tasting the last drippings for salt. I had finished rinsing out the bucket and cartridge covers, and was ready to collect the first water, when a sharp pull came on the bow line, twisting the raft around. Out of the corner of my eye I saw Cherry's raft being rolled over on its beam ends by a wave.

All three men were thrown out, and with Reynolds so weak I was sure he was going to drown. But in the next flash of lightning I counted three heads bobbing around the sides. While they clung to the hand line around the sides, we pulled in the line, bringing them in on our lee side, holding the raft steady while they helped each other in. Reynolds, gasping, mustered the strength to haul himself back. I shall never stop marveling at the hidden resources of men whose minds never give up. Cherry and Whittaker saved the oars, but they saved little else. The Very pistol and the last of the cartridges were lost. So were the bailing bucket and the little water they had collected.

All this—from the breaking away of the little raft to the righting of Cherry's—took no more than ten minutes, perhaps as little as five. But rather than wearing us down the exertions seemed to fill us with strength. I passed Cherry the bailing bucket, and while he bailed I watched anxiously for any letup in the rain. Adamson and Bartek sucked at the wet cloths, filling their mouths with the first water in eight days. To make up for his lost bucket, we gave Cherry the cartridge cover.

When they finally pulled away, I fell to wringing the sopping garments Bartek and Adamson had ready for me. Lightning flashed, the sea rumbled, the raft tossed wildly, but I was not really aware of them. My hands were terribly burned and blistered, and the flesh cracked and the blood spurted out, but I never felt it. As fast as I could wring out the cloths I handed them back to the others, who spread them out to soak again. I was gauging matters by just one thing—the water level in the bailing bucket.

Quite suddenly the wind died down and the rain stopped. The squall could not have lasted more than twenty minutes. But I had nearly a quart and a half of water in the bucket. Cherry, in his boat, had about a quart, but De Angelis and Alex, who had nothing to catch water in, had none. They had simply sucked their shirts.

In the calm that followed, the rafts were pulled in close. The round-table decision was that we'd better try to go on with as little water as possible—a half jigger per man per day. In the dark I poured what I guessed to be that much into one of the empty Very cartridge cases, and passed it seven times down the line of hands. It was the sweetest water I ever tasted. And the rain that had drenched our bodies, washing away the salt rime and cleansing the sores, had refreshed us quite as much.

On the ninth morning we shared the second fish and another half jigger of water. From this point on my memory may be hazy. Alex got no better, and on the tenth day, for his safety and Adamson's, we increased the water ration to two jiggers a day, one in the morning and one at sundown. On the following day we added another at noon.

The weather now took a change, and the sea turned rougher. The three of us in the middle boat had the worst of it, due to the yawing action from the pulls of the raft ahead and the raft behind. As each raft rose to a swell at a different interval, a shock would come on the lines and then would twist our raft first one way, then another. The little raft, being lighter, would coast down a swell and smack us, drenching us with salt water.

This was terribly hard on Adamson, and I insisted that the front raft exchange position with us for a few hours. This was done. It was much smoother. After Adamson had had a few hours' comfort, we returned to our original position in the middle of the line.

It was on the tenth evening, I think, that I asked Bartek to change rafts with Sergeant Alex, thinking that Alex might rest better. It took the combined strength of Bartek, De Angelis, and myself to move him. I stretched him on the lee side on the bottom of the boat and put my arm around him, as a mother cuddles a child, hoping in that way to transfer the heat of my body to him during the night. In an hour or so his shivering stopped and

sleep came—a shallow sleep in which Alex mumbled in-
termittently in Polish—phrases about his mother and his
girl "Snooks."

I kept Alex there all night, the next day and night, and
the twelfth day. He was weaker, although more rational.
When evening came, after the customary prayer, he
asked to be put back in the little boat with De Angelis.
I knew he couldn't last many hours longer, and so we
pulled the other boat up and changed around again. We
had to lift him like a baby. A strong wind came up and
I slept fitfully that night, worrying about that little raft
bouncing on the rough sea. Yet I must have dozed off,
because my next recollection is of the sound of a long
sigh.

I called to De Angelis: "Has he died?"

De Angelis said, after a pause, "I think so."

It was about 3:00 A.M. and very dark, and although it
was hard on De Angelis to wait for dawn with a dead
man across his body, I did not want to make a decision
until there was light to see by. The other men stirred,
woke up, and understood, almost without being told,
what had happened. I remember someone saying, "Well,
his sufferings are over." I think we were all a little
frightened, with the wind blowing and clouds rushing
across the sky, and Alex dead in that plunging raft.
Somewhere I have read that sharks can sense the coming
of death. That night there seemed twice as many as we
had seen before.

At daybreak Bartek hauled Alex' little raft alongside, and Cherry paddled up in his. The body was already stiff, but I checked the heart, the pulse, checked in every way I knew. And I asked Cherry and Whittaker to do so, not wishing to accept the responsibility alone. We agreed Alex was dead. We removed his wallet and identification disc, which Captain Cherry has since returned to the family, and we saved the jacket. De Angelis murmured what he remembered of the Catholic burial service. Then we rolled the body over the side. It did not sink at once but rather floated off face down a little while.

This was the thirteenth morning.

# CHAPTER III

# The Rescue

IT HAD BEEN MY HABIT, as soon as it was light enough to see, to count heads in the rafts. Seven (not including myself) was the number fixed in my mind. At times during the next few days, as I counted automatically, I would discover with a kind of shock that there were only six. Then I would remember. Alex was the seventh.

Alex' death left De Angelis alone in the two-man raft at the end of the line. Bartek asked De Angelis to change places with him. De Angelis was willing, but he preferred to be with his fellow officers in the head raft. So Sergeant Reynolds came back with me and Adamson, and Bartek shifted to the little raft. It did not occur to me to ask him why he wanted to change. He was getting pretty weak, and I assumed he would rest better alone.

Before daylight a morning or two later I woke up to find the little raft gone. The connecting rope was trailing in the water and, having tied the knot myself, I knew it could not have pulled loose.

At daybreak we saw his raft only half a mile away, bobbing up and down on a gentle swell. We waved and yelled. Finally Bartek heard us and paddled back, almost reluctantly. I asked what happened. He admitted having untied the line during the night. I have never been able to understand why and, although I asked him directly, he offered no explanation. He said he didn't know; he didn't know why.

My memory may be a little off, but I think we finished the last of the rain water the evening before Alex died. Another calm spell settled over our piece of the Pacific. The rafts, scarcely moving, lay bunched together, and the sun started to burn our guts out all over again.

We went another forty-eight hours or so without water. After the last drop had gone, several men were almost raving wild in their thirstiness. There is really no limit to what men will try in their extremity. In the first terrible week we had saved our urine in the empty Very cartridge shells and let it stand for several days, hoping that the sun and air would work a beneficial chemical change. That was my idea. It was a bad one.

We had been without food since we ate the last fish on the ninth day. Cherry, who had been fishing patiently, lost the second and last line and hook on a big shark. But before this happened he had actually hooked a two-foot shark. With Whittaker's help, he managed to hoist it into the raft, where he stabbed it with a knife. Cherry cut the carcass into two pieces, keeping the smaller one for his raft and passing the other back to me, for Adamson, Reynolds, and myself, and for Bartek in the little raft.

I cut off equal pieces for the four. The meat was rubbery and tough; it took all my strength to force the rusty blade through it. Maybe we were more pernickety than some other castaways, but hungry as we were, no one had stomach for shark meat. It had a foul, rancid taste and the two or three of us who chewed and sucked the meat, mostly for the liquid in it, soon spit out the pieces, gagging as we did so. I kept my piece in the boat all day, hoping the sun would cure it and make it palatable, but I simply could not down it. When I offered them another piece, Adamson and Bartek shook their heads. The flesh was beginning to stink, so I threw it overboard, without regret. In a little while I heard a splash—Cherry's half had followed ours.

The sharks were around us all the time as I have already said. Whether it was because they scented food on the rafts or whether they resented these unfamiliar objects, or even because they were trying to dislodge the leeches on their backs, they kept attacking us. They would come up under the boat and hit the bottom a vicious jolt; so hard, in fact, that it would be raised several inches from the water. They did this with their mouths, which are round. Fortunately, the boat was taut and they could not get their teeth into it. We comforted ourselves with the thought that we were safe from that peril until later we discovered a series of tiny jagged breaks on the bottom of all the boats. They looked as though they had been caused by the bottom teeth of our untiring enemies. Another disturbing habit they had was to come up day and night and slap the sides of the boats with their tails, showering us with water.

While trying to stab the shark in the raft, Cherry had driven his knife through the rubberized canvas floor, making a quarter-inch tear, through which water seeped. Because the day was calm, Cherry decided to try to make a patch with the repair kit. In the kit were a tube of glue, a piece of sandpaper, and a small roll of patching material. The problem was to dry the raft bottom so the patch would hold. Cherry and the other two got out of their raft and turned it bottom side up, so that it floated on the inflated roll, leaving an air space underneath. Then they hauled themselves back on the bottom, resting there while the canvas dried.

The patch was a failure—perhaps because the patching material was ruined by salt water. It pulled loose soon after they righted the raft. They never tried another. The rent didn't let in enough water to be dangerous, but enough to make them miserable. Unless they bailed frequently, there was always two or three inches of water in the bottom.

That was bad, not just because it was uncomfortable, but also because the salt sores that covered them never

had a chance to heal. We all had them, and in many ways
they caused the most pain. First there was an evil-looking
rash that spread over the thighs and bumpus. Then the
sores would come—hard, angry red things, full of pus,
that looked like boils and hurt worse. When they broke,
they left running sores which never seemed to dry.

Our bodies, our minds, the few things we had with us
were slowly rotting away. All the watches except Whittaker's stopped running, as salt-water corrosion froze the
works. The compass needle ceased to point and finally
rusted hard in the direction in which it had set. The silver
coins in my pockets took on a discolored look. The secret
orders that Mr. Stimson had given me faded and became
unintelligible. The colors and the print came off our
only map, which finally stuck together at the folds and
could not be opened. But by then I had memorized the
position of every island or bit of land of any possible
use to us.

In the breast pocket of my coat I have carried, for
many years, a little leather case containing a crucifix and
three St. Christopher medals. The crucifix was given to
me in 1917 when I left with the A.E.F. by a ten-year-old
girl, the daughter of a friend. Whenever I flew on the
Western Front, I always had that case in my flying suit.
As the case wore out I had it replaced—half-a-dozen
times, I'd say. It was with me the night I flew into a hill
near Atlanta. And it was with me again on the Pacific.
Like all the other metal things, the crucifix and the

medals started to corrode and disintegrate. I am not a Catholic and, aside from the sentiment connected with such things, I was certainly under no illusions as to what they could do for me. Yet after all the years, and the good fortune associated with them, I found myself believing, as men will when everything else is going to pieces, that my fate was somehow involved with them.

The watch I had was a gift from the city of Detroit after World War I. It was a fine, expensive timepiece; I valued it for that and other reasons. Yet not to be able to tell the time turned out to be no particular loss. Time, merely as something to keep track of, ceased to be any real concern of ours. One of the men who had a small notebook kept a diary through the first week but as far as I could see he never wrote afterward.

Adamson used to pencil terse notes on the side of the raft, with the date. But by the second week he was satisfied merely to scratch the day. His last note I remember clearly:

"Fourteenth day. Rick and I still alive."

Either the fourteenth night, or the night before, an unexpected and depressing event occurred. After Alex died, I began to despair of Adamson. The nagging pain in his back, aggravated by salt-water sores, gave him no peace. To my knowledge he never slept deeply. He just slipped off into a permanent semi-consciousness, occasionally broken by feeble gusts of fury and intolerable pain. His feet, legs, arms, wrists, and face had been burned to a red pulp and any movement in the raft, however slight, was certain to communicate itself to his back.

Hans Adamson is an old and dear friend. It was a terrible responsibility to sit there and watch the strength go out of him. His clothes were rotting on his back. The colonel's eagles on his tunic were corroded. His uniform shirt and pants were water-stained and coming to pieces. A gray stubble covered his face, and his eyes were blood-shot and swollen.

On this particular night I felt the raft give a violent lurch. My first thought was that a shark was attacking. Adamson's body was no longer against mine. His end of the raft was empty. I saw something struggling in the water close by and my hand gripped Adamson's shoulder. He was too heavy for me to hold up alone, but my yells for help brought Cherry and Whittaker up in their raft. We were a long time at it, but we managed to haul him back into the raft.

In the morning Hans had a long, lucid interval. We talked about many things, familiar and pleasant things done together, the mission we were on. But from that day on he seldom spoke or asked for anything.

It does us no dishonor to say that we were all becoming a little unhinged. We were unreasonable, at times, in our demands upon one another. Wrathful and profane words were exchanged over nothing at all. Every night the rafts were drawn together for prayer meeting. We continued to read from Bartek's New Testament, now yellowed and stained by salt water. But one or two, who had been most fervent, became backsliders. Because their prayers were not answered within twenty-four or forty-eight hours, they condemned the Lord for His failure to save them. They wanted deliverance immediately.

I tried to impart my own philosophy to these men, hoping to stimulate their desire to carry on. It was based upon the simple observation that the longer I have had to suffer under trying circumstances, the more certain I was to appreciate my deliverance. That is part of the wisdom that comes to older men.

If that didn't work, I would turn to the only other weapon left, and that was to brutalize and jar those whose chins sagged too far down on their chests. One man said to me across twenty feet of water: "Rickenbacker, you are the meanest, most cantankerous so-and-so that ever lived." Some of the things I said could have been a heavy weight on my conscience. But I felt better after we reached land. Several of the boys confessed that they once swore an oath to live for the sheer pleasure of burying me at sea.

There were occasions when I myself was pretty hard pressed: when my private store of aches and pains reduced me to something less than a good companion. My legs and hip were rather severely torn in the Atlanta crash. Right up to the time of the Pacific trip I was under regular diathermic and physiotherapeutic treatment. If anyone had told me I could live for twenty-one days with two other men in a space approximately nine feet by five, I would have said he was crazy.

As I got thinner and thinner, my teeth began to give trouble. The gums seemed to shrink in proportion to the rest of me, and the new front bridgework which my dentist finished a few days before I left turned loose and uncomfortable. My mouth dried out, and under the bridge the saliva formed an evil-tasting, cottony substance that felt like mush. However, by washing the bridge four and five times a day in the ocean, and forcing salt water against the gums with my tongue, I found some relief. Knowing the fix I'd be in if the bridge ever slipped out of my hand, I was extremely cautious about this ceremony—overcautious, in fact. One time it did slip from my hand, but I had it back before it had sunk six inches. For me that was the most frightening moment in the twenty-one days.

Naturally, as time went on, the days grew longer. We could see moving objects, we could see each other, we could see the waves breaking, and the swells of the ocean. Sometimes we would see seagulls, and always they raised false hopes that we were near land. I should have known better; I have crossed most of the oceans of the world and found gulls everywhere and at all distances from land.

The nights grew more deadly. Some of the boys would talk in their sleep, others would cry out in nightmares, and at times I could hear some of them praying. Each

VICTORY OVER DEATH and ultimate victory for our cause are reflected in Captain Rickenbacker's smile as he lands in San Francisco on December seventeenth. Under strict orders, he was guarded by an Army escort.

AT THE MERCY OF WIND AND RAIN, SUN AND WEATHER, Captain
Rickenbacker drifted for twenty-one days in tiny rubber life rafts like these.

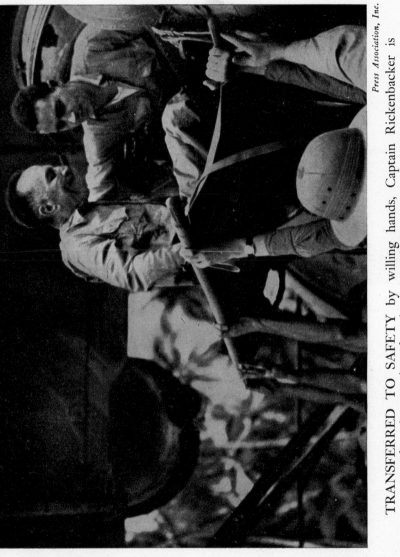

TRANSFERRED TO SAFETY by willing hands, Captain Rickenbacker is moved to the rescuing plane by a stretcher.

CAPTAIN WILLIAM T. CHERRY, JR.

COLONEL HANS C. ADAMSON.

LIEUTENANT JOHN J. DE ANGELIS.

PRIVATE JOHN F. BARTEK.

*Courtesy of Dmitri Kessel*

CAPTAIN RICKENBACKER.

*Press Association, Inc.*

LIEUTENANT JAMES C. WHITTAKER.

*Press Association, Inc.*

SERGEANT JAMES W. REYNOLDS.

*Press Association, Inc.*

STAFF SERGEANT ALEXANDER
KACZMARCZYK (*died at sea*).

*Press Association, Inc.*

SECRETARY OF WAR HENRY L. STIMSON claps a
hand on the shoulder of Captain Rickenbacker as the
famous flier reports in Washington, December nineteenth.

THE SENATE, TOO, is eager to hear the story of those twenty-one incredible days on a life raft.

"WE CAN NEVER APPROXIMATE THE SACRIFICES our men are making on the battle front."

period, from darkness to daylight, seemed like eternity. Always I kept trying to think and rack my brain for a way out of our dilemma. I had never lost my belief that we would be found. How, where, or when, was what I was trying to think through.

I had one hope and wish since we were drifting southwest, that a violent storm might come up and catch us in its clutches and carry us at a much greater rate of speed into some island haven.

So hard did I think of the many possibilities that during the last few nights, and particularly from midnight until dawn when the mist was at its worst, I would doze off and dream of having landed on an island where I found an old friend with a lovely home who was happy and glad to welcome us, and who put me up in a nice soft bed and gave me a most delicious breakfast, with an abundance of fruit juices which I craved. And after breakfast, all I had to do was to wait until Mr. Stimson, Secretary of War, arrived at his office. My friend in these dreams had a telephone, and I could reach Secretary Stimson directly, telling him where we were.

Then as the gray dawn came over the horizon, I would awaken to find to my horror and amazement that I was still on the broad Pacific, with its thick mist and that everlasting rocking to and fro that goes with the ocean swells.

Even after we were picked up, for many, many nights in the hospital I would awaken with that same hallucination and dream, with the everlasting rocking and swinging of the raft under me.

Both Cherry and I were convinced we were well to the north and west of the convoy and air-ferry routes. We tried from time to time to paddle in a southeasterly direction, but the efforts taxed us and we gave up. It seemed much more important to conserve our strength.

Naturally, during all these days of drifting, we did not go in the same direction. Sometimes the squalls would drive us in the opposite direction for hours at a time. Always, however, the tendency was to the southwest. This meant that we would see the squalls coming up from behind and at first we were afraid they would miss us. We would paddle like the devil in their direction, hoping to get into their path. They traveled so much faster than we could that we often missed them. We all got to be experts in knowing which one was going to come our way and which was not.

On the fourteenth night or so we got a wonderful break. A series of squalls, one behind the other, passed over the rafts. It was a wild night. I doubt if I have ever worked so hard, or to such good effect. When I finished wringing the last shirt and sock dry at dawn, there was a gallon of water in my bailing bucket. Cherry had nearly as much in the Mae West. In the morning and again at noon we had a jigger around. This, with what we had sucked from the clothes before we squeezed the water out, refreshed and heartened us.

But because our last resources were plainly running out, we held council the next afternoon and decided to chance a course that I had steadily held to be risky. Ever since leaving the airplane I had insisted that the rafts stay together. But now I had come to believe that our only hope was for one raft, manned by the strongest three, to try to beat across the current to the southeast. In that direction they stood a better chance to fall in with a transport plane or a ship; and if they were lucky enough to be picked up alive, they would direct the search for us. Cherry agreed to go, and Whittaker and De Angelis, who were in better shape than any of the others, also volunteered. I gave them most of the water and the last oar in the little raft.

They set out in the early afternoon. Or I should say they tried to set out. They untied the line and paddled off. The sea was flat, but there was a slight head wind. Hours later they were still in sight, not more than a mile away, perhaps less. Watching, I could see two men paddling while the third rested. Long after the sun had set, I saw their shadows rising on the swell. Then I lost them in the night mist.

When day came and I hauled myself over Reynolds' back for a look around I saw they were only a short distance away, sleeping. Presently they paddled back, exhausted. Cherry said it was a physical impossibility to force the raft against the current and that little breeze. This was a heavy disappointment to all of us, but in an odd way the incident marked a turning point in our fortunes. Thereafter we were never without water. The skies clouded over, and there were few hours during the day or night when rain squalls were not chasing across the horizon.

We also invented a storage system for water. I hated to leave it in the bailing bucket on the bottom of the raft because there was always the risk of knocking it over. And the loss by evaporation during the heat of the day could be very heavy. The idea of using the Mae West life jacket, which I wore, occurred to me. This had two double compartments, filled with carbon dioxide, each closed by a bicycle valve.

I let out the gas and, taking a mouthful at a time from the bailing bucket, forced the water down a narrow tube past the valve into the compartment. This took a long time—perhaps fifteen to twenty minutes to transfer a quart. All the while the boys had their eyes fixed on my Adam's apple, watching for a convulsive jerk. The honor system has seldom been put to a more severe test, and I can't blame the others for being suspicious. One night I heard one man muttering to a companion that while it only took a count of three for Rickenbacker to fill his mouth from the bucket, it took a count of sixteen for him to transfer the mouthful to the jacket.

The three empty Very cartridges that we had saved served as drinking cups. They were about six inches long and perhaps an inch and a quarter wide. There was one in each raft. Proving how far men will go in adapting themselves to hard conditions, we also urinated in them since we dared not stand up in the raft. (Throughout the twenty-one days, even when we were without water, our kidneys functioned almost normally. On the other hand, I do not recall that anyone had a single bowel movement.)

With water we also gained a little food, by a great stroke of luck. One night in the third week there was a tremendous splashing all around the boat. It was pitch dark, but the water blazed with zigzagging phosphorescent streaks. We could hear heavy bodies hitting the water terrific smacks.

A pack of sharks had hit a school of mackerel with the rafts in the middle of the slaughter. The terrified mackerel shot out of the water like star shells. One landed in my raft and I fell on him before he could flop out. Simultaneously another landed in Cherry's boat and was bagged. They provided food for two days. It was our first in nearly a week.

Cherry was the only one who could claim to have been hurt by a shark, and this was by mistake. One time we were all aroused by a bloodcurdling shriek. There was a God-awful thrashing around in the forward raft and finally I heard Cherry yelling, "A damn shark came up and hit me and broke my nose."

We pulled the boats together and from Cherry's misery it was plain that he had been hit a hard wallop.

Blood was streaming down his face and shirt. Whittaker made him lie down while he heaped wet handkerchiefs over his nose. This stopped the bleeding and, after the pain eased, Cherry decided that his nose hadn't been broken after all. He had only the foggiest idea how it happened. He was stretched across the raft, with the upper half of his body across the inflated bulge, and while asleep he must have rolled out, just far enough for a shark to reach him with a flick of the tail.

The seventeenth day brought the first tantalizing hint that we had finally drifted within the reach of assistance. We had been through several days and nights of squally weather which blew us in all directions. The rafts had taken a pounding, and the interminable slap-slap of the waves, the everlasting pitching and swaying, had left us sleepless, exhausted, and miserable. I would wring rain water from clothes until my fingers turned stiff and useless. Then I would rest and wring some more. The reserve in the Mae West grew steadily; it had a fine heft when I lifted it. And we were drinking three jiggers a day per man.

This particular afternoon was heavily overcast; the sea was quite rough, with whitecaps, and I was worrying about the strain on the connecting lines. I saw Cherry in the raft ahead sit up and cock his head. Then he shouted back, "I hear a plane. Listen!"

In a few minutes we all saw an airplane off to the left. It came out of a squall, flying low and fast, about five miles away. Bartek was back in my raft that day. He stood up while I held him, and waved his arms and shouted until he slid out of my arms and fell exhausted across the raft.

The seven of us yelled our lungs out. The plane came no nearer. It was a single-engine pontoon job. I doubt that we had it in sight more than three or four minutes. It was too far off for us to make out its markings. A squall moved in between and we did not see it again. The yelling stopped, and for a long time no one talked. My throat hurt from shouting so much.

Yet just to see that airplane was a terrific stimulus. It was the first outside sign of human life visible to us in two and a half weeks. Here at last was proof that land was close by, or at least a ship capable of catapulting such an airplane. Only the sick men slept that night. Cherry, Whittaker, De Angelis, and I talked steadily across the rafts.

On the eighteenth day, again in the afternoon, we saw two more airplanes of the same type, flying close together, perhaps six miles away. We waved our shirts but did not shout, knowing it was useless. On the nineteenth day, in the morning, there were four more airplanes, first a pair to the north, then another to the south, perhaps 4,000 feet high. First the strong, resonant note of the engines came from below the horizon; then we saw the planes themselves; then we watched them disappear. The sound lingered after they had gone.

That afternoon no airplanes appeared and somehow the fear took hold of us that perhaps we had gone past the land, perhaps we had drifted through a string of islands and were moving into the open Pacific. Being picked up, quite obviously, was going to be a chance in a million. We had assumed that an airplane with a vigilant crew could not miss the bright yellow rafts. Now we knew otherwise. In a rough sea the rafts must be just flecks against the whitecaps.

Yet this should have been our best time. We had water in reserve and we also had food. In the early morning, in the gray half light before dawn, hundreds and hundreds of finger-length fish, resembling sardines, collected around the rafts. With practice and diligence we learned how to scoop them up. The trick was to bring your hand from behind and pin them with a quick move against the raft. But for every one landed, a hundred were lost. Through the last three days we must have caught between twenty and thirty. They were divided, share and share alike, and the fishes were still wriggling when we bit into them. I crunched them and downed them whole.

We came to the evening of the twentieth day—about six o'clock. Cherry and De Angelis were arguing. I paid no attention until a phrase, louder than the others, came across the little stretch of water. It was the first inkling of what was afoot. Captain Cherry wanted De Angelis to give up his place in the little raft. "Why do you want it, Cherry?" I asked. He answered, "I'm going to try to make land. Staying together is no good. They'll never see us this way."

I told Cherry then he was wrong, and I still think he was wrong, despite the fact he was the first to be picked up. We argued back and forth between the rafts for at least an hour. My point was that he had no way of telling which was the best direction to take. The various airplanes had appeared in the north, south, east, and west. And if they couldn't see three rafts bunched together, what chance did they have of seeing one? But Cherry was insistent. He argued that our only chance was to scatter. Yet he left the decision to me, saying: "I won't go unless you agree it is all right for me to."

I realized that no good would come out of prolonging the argument. De Angelis paddled past us in the little raft, transferred to the lead raft, and Cherry took his place. I wished Captain Cherry well and said so long. He had some water in his Mae West, so I was not worried on that account. He drifted off alone, carried by the swell and a slight breeze.

Whittaker and De Angelis watched the receding raft with increasing nervousness. I heard them saying that maybe Cherry was right and there was nothing to be gained by staying together. They, too, decided to go off. I remonstrated with them as I had with Cherry. I was angry now. "What about Reynolds?" I said. "You haven't asked him." They couldn't ask him, Reynolds was too sick, too weak, to understand.

I gave in again. The talk had worn me down.

Cherry was almost out of sight when Whittaker cast off the line. Both rafts were out of sight before night fell. Now there were three of us—Adamson, Bartek, and myself. Adamson and Bartek were more dead than alive. They hadn't been drawn into the arguments of the afternoon. I doubt that they even heard what was said. They were scrunched up at opposite ends of the raft.

I was terribly worried that night. If we had indeed drifted past land, our chances of holding out much longer were damn poor. I had perhaps two quarts and a pint of water in the Mae West. Half of this, in one compartment, was good, sweet water. The rest was dubious, being from the first wringing of the soaked rags. To be sure of getting rid of all the salt in the rags we had at first thrown away the first pint or so, after using it to rinse out the bailing bucket and the Very cartridge cases. However, a sip convinced me this water was drinkable and thereafter I frugally transferred the first water of a rain to the inside compartment of the Mae West. This became the emergency supply. The product of subsequent wringings went into what I called the "sweet-water" chamber. This provided the regular ration.

On the twenty-first morning I woke from a particularly pleasant version of my usual dream. I issued the morning jigger of water, but Adamson and Bartek were almost too weak to raise their heads to drink. As I measured the water into the shell, my hand trembled so much

I spilled some. Part of Bartek's ration ran down his chin, and I had to give him more to make up for it. After two hours of scooping I caught several more of the little fishes. But I was nervous and impatient and my hand moved with exasperating clumsiness.

The sky had cleared during the night and after the sun got up it turned terribly hot. I watched for seaweed and debris—anything suggestive of land. But the ocean was bare. Even the gulls were absent. Some time during the morning Bartek emerged briefly from his coma and asked: "Have the planes come back?"

I said, "No, there haven't been any since day before yesterday."

He seemed to have difficulty understanding this. Then he mumbled, "They won't come back. I know. They won't come back." He said that over and over again.

Yet it was Bartek who first heard the planes when they returned late in the afternoon. I am quite sure that I was awake, but my senses must have been dulled, because Bartek pulled at my shirt and whispered, "Listen, Captain —planes! They're back. They're very near."

There were two airplanes approaching from the southeast. Adamson and Bartek were too weak to stand themselves, or to hold me up. Sitting down, I waved as hard as I could with my old hat. The planes, only a few hundred yards off the water, passed within a couple of miles and disappeared into the setting sun. My first elation was swallowed up in despair. Night was only a few hours away. This was our last chance.

clean and handsome they were, how proud I was to have them as countrymen.

They introduced themselves—Lieutenant Eadie (W. F. Eadie of Evanston, Illinois) and Radioman Boutte (L. H. Boutte of Abbeville, Louisiana). Eadie said a PT boat was on its way to take us in. But he went on to say that he didn't want to show another light, since there might be Japs in the vicinity. So rather than wait, he proposed that we taxi into the base, which he said was forty miles away.

I told the lieutenant that first we had to dispose of a piece of unfinished business. The afternoon before, after the others had gone off, I had made this deal with Bartek and Adamson: the moment we knew we were safe, all the water in the Mae West was to be divided. They were to have all the sweet water and I the "tainted." This would give me twice as much water, but they were all for it.

I opened the valve in the Mae West and poured the sweet water into the bailing bucket for Adamson and Bartek. There was enough to give each a pint. While they were drinking, I unscrewed the other valve, lifted the tube to my lips, and drank to the last drop. I must have had nearly a quart. It was salty all right, but if there had been a gallon I would have taken it.

Lieutenant Eadie meanwhile gave us the good news about the others. Captain Cherry had been sighted the afternoon before about twenty-five miles away by a

Navy plane on routine evening patrol, piloted by Lieutenant Frederick E. Woodward of Davenport, Iowa. With him was the same radioman who was with Eadie, and he was first to sight the raft.

Luckily for Cherry, a PT boat was near by. Cherry, not knowing where we had drifted during the night, was able to give only vague directions as to our likely position. Every available plane was put in the air, and in the midst of the search a radio call from a near-by island informed the base that natives had seen three castaways on the beach of an uninhabited island several miles away. This news was supplied by an English missionary who had a small radio transmitter, and presumably it accounted for Whittaker, De Angelis, and Reynolds. A doctor had already been dispatched to them in an airplane.

We were really the lucky ones. Our raft, during the night, drifted through the chain of islands into the open sea. The next landfall was hundreds of miles away. There is, of course, no way of telling how far we drifted during the twenty-one days. My guess is between four hundred and five hundred miles. Unknowingly, we had drifted across the International Date Line, losing a day. By our calendar we were picked up Wednesday, November 11— or Thursday, November 12, by the pilot's. We were then a few hours into our twenty-second day.

After we had finished the water, Eadie and Boutte hoisted Adamson eight feet into the cockpit. The plane had room for only one passenger and I took it for granted that Eadie would leave Bartek and me behind. So I said to Lieutenant Eadie, "Would you mind waiting until the PT does come up? I don't want them to miss us in the dark."

Eadie said calmly, "Why, Captain Eddie, you fellows are going too."

I looked at the cockpit. "Where?" He smiled and said, "On the wing."

Eadie had the strength of Hercules. With Boutte's help he hauled Bartek to the wing, lifted him over the cockpit, and sat him on the right wing with his legs hanging over the leading edge. In that position he was tied securely to the wing and cockpit. I was boosted to the left wing and tied in the same way. I was deeply impressed by these two young Navy fliers. They knew their business, they asked no foolish questions. All that we could say was "This is heaven," and "Thank God," and "God bless the Navy."

I don't know how long we taxied—perhaps half an hour. It was pitch dark and with the propeller wash battering my eyelids I couldn't see much anyway. Presently the shadow of a PT boat loomed up ahead. Eadie cut the engine and drifted within hailing distance. After a three-cornered argument involving him, the skipper of the PT boat, and myself, it was arranged that Bartek and I be transferred and that Adamson continue in the plane rather than be put to the discomfort of another change.

It was no hardship for me to change. I knew there'd be water and food—but water, above all—on the boat. They lowered Bartek and me back into the raft, and I paddled across to the boat. Planting my feet upon an American deck was the next-best thing to being home. The crew gave us a cheer. It bucked us up no end, but we hardly deserved it. There's no great honor attached to saving your own skin.

Bed rolls and blankets were laid out. Bartek fell asleep instantly, but all the excitement made me wakeful. Moreover, the salty water I had drunk stimulated a bowel action that took me to the toilet. My legs were rusty after days and nights of just sitting. Nevertheless, by holding on to things I managed to get to the washroom.

Water was the only thing on my mind. One of the men led me into a cabin where I downed four China mugs of water in quick succession. The skipper, who was barely half my age, became alarmed. "Aren't you overdoing it?" he asked. I said yes, maybe too much water would be bad. So I had a couple of mugs of pineapple juice and a mug of hot beef broth, one after the other.

By this time we were at the base, and a beaching boat had come alongside. A Colonel Fuller, the ranking doctor, appeared with several pharmacist's mates. They had two stretchers, on which they lowered Bartek and me to the other boat. A few minutes later the keel crunched on the beach. We were carried across the beach and down a road, under the most beautiful palm trees I have ever seen. The moon was shining through the clouds, the air was warm—it was a lovely evening.

They took us into a little one-story hospital, with eight or ten cots in a single room. Colonel Fuller said proudly it had just been built and we were the first patients. My clothes literally came apart as they undressed me. As soon as they put me to bed, I demanded water. The colonel turned to the pharmacist's mate and directed him to give me two ounces every two hours. I said I wanted it in a bucket, not a medicine dropper. "If you drink too much," the colonel said, "the aftereffects could be quite serious." I told him what I had had on the PT boat. "All the more reason," he said severely. "Two ounces every two hours."

That was all I got and that night I was literally afire. I thirsted as I never had the worst day on the raft. The salt in the water I had drunk was doubtless responsible.

I slept badly. The burns on my wrists, neck, and face, the loathsome sores that covered my legs, thighs, and bumpus were plastered with healing compounds, but they hurt now as they never hurt on the raft. My old dream repeated itself, but with a nightmarish twist at the end. I was again in that fine house, eating and drinking with gluttonous pleasure. Then the dream dissolved and I woke almost in terror, imagining the raft was rocking and swinging under me, and mistaking the moonlight through the windows for the ocean mist.

In the morning I was aroused by a fearful hammering

and pounding. I was told that a new and bigger hospital was being built a short distance away. Cherry was brought in that day and on the following day Whittaker and De Angelis arrived. After being picked up, they had all been taken aboard a Navy tender. Poor Reynolds, however, had to be left behind. In his weakened condition the doctors were afraid to move him. I found I had lost forty pounds on the raft. Adamson and Cherry, both heavier than I to start with, had each lost fifty-five pounds.

Whittaker and De Angelis had a hair-raising tale to tell. The morning after they left us they saw palm trees a long way off to the north. Whittaker said he rowed for hours. Every approach to the island was guarded by reefs, over which the surf broke heavily, but they took a chance and rode the breakers to the beach. Too weak to walk, Whittaker and De Angelis crawled on their hands and knees, dragging Reynolds between them.

After propping Reynolds against a palm tree, they searched the underbrush for food and water. A short distance away they found a partly finished hut and the half-finished hull of a canoe, carved from the trunk of a coconut tree. The canoe had collected considerable rain water. They skimmed off the dead bugs and drank to their bellies' content. The rubbish was infested with rats. They got close enough to one to club it to death, and devoured it raw. Afterward some natives arrived in a canoe and took them to an island several miles away.

Here they were cared for by the English missionary until the Navy doctor arrived.

That same afternoon a flying boat brought two doctors in from Samoa—a Captain Jacobs of the Marine Corps and a Lieutenant Commander Durkin of the Navy. They gave us a careful going over and decided that all of us, except Bartek, should fly back with them to Samoa. Bartek was still too sick to be moved. As for Reynolds, the last word was that it would be best for him to remain on the tender. Adamson had failed to bounce back as rapidly as the rest and the doctors deliberated some time over the wisdom of moving him. They finally decided to chance it, since the base hospital at Samoa was much better equipped to take care of him. It was a good thing they did. Had they left Hans there, I am sure he would have died before another week was out.

In three flying boats we took off early Monday morning. I was mighty glad to be on my way, but I was also sorry to leave my friends on the island. My affection went beyond the fact that they had done so many wonderful things for us. I liked their spirit, the conscientious way they went about their patrols, and I liked the way they put up that hospital. College men for the most part, pharmacist's mates by Navy grade, few of them knew anything about carpentry. But they put up that hospital in three days. They were up before dawn and they worked until dark. There's no forty-hour week on Island Z.

# CHAPTER IV

# Completing the Mission

THE FLIGHT TO SAMOA from Island Z took all day. It was good to be making one hundred and twenty knots or so over the ocean after all those days of pointless drifting. Now we were really getting somewhere and our lives again had a purpose.

About halfway to Samoa the three PBY's stopped at an island under Marine control. This was to allow us to rest and have lunch. The meal was prepared by two wisecracking colored cooks from Georgia. They gave me my first good laugh in a month and the best meal I've ever had. The two doctors with us—Captain Jacobs and Commander Durkin—had ordered a meat soup. They came into the mess hall to see how we were doing and were flabbergasted to find that with the co-operation of the cooks we were just finishing the third bowl and about to begin on the fourth. The doctors called a halt right then and there, but not until the cooks had slipped us two heaping platters of pineapple ice cream.

The rest of the flight was uneventful; we arrived at Samoa before dark and were taken immediately to the base hospital. It is a large and exceptionally fine establishment; it even possesses an air-conditioned operating room.

In these pleasant surroundings Captain Cherry, Lieutenant Whittaker, and Lieutenant De Angelis came back fast. The doctors said the Pacific would leave no lasting marks on their minds and bodies. And I was fortunate enough to possess a rugged constitution that assured me the same kind of recovery. I sent a message to Mr. Stimson, the Secretary of War, saying that I expected to be able to continue with my mission within ten days or two weeks. His answer was most cordial. That same day my friend "Hap" Arnold [Lieutenant General Henry H. Arnold, chief of the Army Air Forces] sent word that as soon as I was ready to go on he would dispatch a transport from the West coast.

My pleasure was spoiled by the sad news concerning Colonel Adamson. The doctors were puzzled by his failure to snap back, until their tests showed up a serious case of diabetes. Hans was as surprised as they were. No doctor who had ever examined him in the past suspected the presence of diabetes, and the Navy doctors could not tell whether his was a dormant case, or whether it had been brought on by a lowering of the metabolism as a result of starvation. Actually, as we have found out since, it was the latter. Though still a sick man, Adamson today has no trace of diabetes.

The base hospital was without insulin, but it so happened that aboard a ship which arrived that same day was an Army doctor, a chronic diabetic, who possessed an ample supply. As he was returning to the States, he generously left for Hans all but the minimum amount required to sustain him the rest of the voyage. This was enough to keep Hans going until more could be flown from the States.

Adamson's misfortunes, however, were not yet over. A few days later he came down with pneumonia; the doctors had to work night and day to save him. They resorted to one of the most powerful of the sulfa drugs, which itself produced a peculiar and alarming reaction. If I understood the doctors correctly, this drug has the effect, upon one patient out of five hundred, of breaking down the red blood corpuscles; it was Hans's bad luck to be that one. His red blood count fell off rapidly. Three transfusions were made in rapid succession, with blood contributed by the hospital attendants.

There was no chance now of his continuing the mission with me. But I couldn't bring myself to tell him. I could see the question mark in his eyes, and although he never asked me directly when I was leaving, and whether I expected to go on alone, I knew from the attendants that he was always asking if I'd ever mentioned my plans.

The two weeks at Samoa fixed me up fine. I drank gallons and gallons of fruit juices, and I ate everything put before me. I put back twenty pounds of the forty pounds I had lost on the raft, and to get back in shape I had persuaded the commanding general to let me tour the island. There's nothing like a jeep for hardening you up.

Military rules prevent me from saying much about this Samoan base. I can only say that when I was there it was alive with all kinds of military activities; and from being one of those so-called island paradises of the South Seas it was fast becoming an ocean fortress. The scenery is wonderful, and in many other respects the South Seas is the most attractive place in the world to fight a war. But the region has its drawbacks. The rainy season had just begun, and you have my word for it, it doesn't just rain out there—the ocean tilts up and swamps you. Within a week or so Bartek was flown down from Island Z. Although still terribly emaciated, he was getting his strength back. He brought news of Sergeant Reynolds, who was still too sick to be moved, but quite out of danger.

Toward the last of the month I was well enough to call for the airplane that General Arnold had promised. It arrived Sunday afternoon, November 29. I made arrangements to leave for Australia the following Tuesday morning, after the crew had rested. Monday afternoon I had the unhappy chore of telling Hans Adamson that

I was leaving him behind. He had already steeled himself for that, since it was no secret to him that he was very sick. But I promised to stop on the way back and take him home, if he did his part and threw off his illness.

I left Samoa December 1 soon after sunrise. The airplane was a Consolidated B-24 bomber, converted for transport duty. It had a crew of six, under Captain H. P. Luna, and I can say that I have never flown with a better team of airmen. Because the distances to be covered were so great, and my time was limited, I arranged my schedule so as to do most of the traveling at night. A cot and sleeping bag were placed in the cabin; they proved restful and comfortable.

Since mine was a secret mission and since many of the bases visited are under censorship, it will be understood that from this point on I can speak only in general terms. My first objective was Australia. On the way, making jumps of eight hundred to one thousand miles, I stopped at various island bases. I met the officers and many of the men—they showed me their equipment and discussed their problems and their troubles. Nearly everywhere I found old friends in new jobs and some who were back at an old trade, among them Colonel Weir Cook, who had been one of the aces of my old squadron, the 94th, in World War I.

Eventually I arrived at Brisbane, Australia. Two messages were waiting for me. One was from Mr. Stimson in Washington. Mr. Stimson said that Prime Minister

Churchill had called him on the transatlantic telephone from London to find out how I was and to wish me well. On my earlier mission to England, as I have said, I met Mr. Churchill by chance at a flying field outside London. That he should remember me and go to the trouble of wishing me well, in the midst of his many heavy responsibilities, proves his greatness, his concern for the humble.

The other message was from General MacArthur, saying that arrangements had been made for me to proceed to his headquarters in New Guinea. But because New Guinea is a battle area, the general refused to let me make the last run in the B-24, which was unarmed. Instead he sent down one of his own B-17's, with a combat crew.

The flight across Torres Strait was made in the day. It left me a little disappointed. I had the old soldier's desire for the smell of powder, and I was hoping a Zero or two—no more—would make a pass, so that I could watch the gunners work on them.

We landed at Port Moresby a little after sundown, in just enough light to see the landing strip. I was immediately taken to a hut where I met two "buddies" of World War I, now staff assistants to Lieutenant General George Kenney, who bosses MacArthur's Air Force. One was Brigadier General Ennis Whitehead, and the other was Brigadier General Kenneth Walker, one of the outstanding heavy-bombardment experts in the United

States Air Forces. They drove me over to General Mac-Arthur's headquarters, and the general, who can be the most cordial man on earth, invited me to be his house guest for the week end.

Port Moresby is the dust bowl of all creation. It's just a harbor and a heap of red dust that is constantly in motion, due to the winds funneling down the passes of the Owen Stanley Range. The heat is awful, and the mosquitoes are worse. It used to be called a city, but after what the Mitsubishi bombers have done, I would hesitate to call it that now. Nothing much is left but ruins and isolated groups of native huts. The smashed, half-sunken hulk of a freighter lay in the harbor.

General MacArthur's headquarters consist of a frame shack and an outhouse containing a cold-water shower that always runs warm. His bedroom opens into the room that serves as combat headquarters. The walls are covered with maps, with pins marking the position of our troops and those of the enemy. For a full general, Mac-Arthur lives anything but pretentiously.

The general was a delightful host. At dinner and during the usual hour of talk that followed he and General Kenney went over the air problems in a frank and searching manner. Out of personal curiosity, I tried to get him to talk about Bataan and Corregidor, but he declined to go beyond a few polite generalizations; all that, quite obviously, has been pushed into the background of his mind. He showed no signs of strain and his physical condition seemed excellent. Whenever I looked he was moving. While dictating, or discussing a problem with his staff, he paces back and forth across the room, hesitating now and then to make a point, or listen to a point being made by one of his staff.

General MacArthur gets up at 6 A.M. for a six forty-five breakfast, and during the three nights I was at Port Moresby he never stopped working before midnight. General Kenney usually sits down with him after dinner and they go over the common problems. What impressed me most about MacArthur was his grasp of the air problem in the Southwest Pacific and his enthusiasm for the fighting and transport airplane. After the Japanese had been forced back through the Owen Stanley Range, and down into Cona and Buna, the air was the only effective route for troops, ammunition, supplies, rations, and guns. All the wounded were moved out by air. A first-class job has been done and MacArthur gives credit to the tremendous achievements of the Air Force under General Kenney, a hardheaded, hard-hitting airman, one of the world's best.

I saw no fighting in New Guinea. The moon was shining, the skies were clear, and General Kenney told me I could expect a visit from the "Nips." But they did not come, probably because they were finding it hard to muster a force under the heavy punishment Kenney's boys were dishing out. Until a week or ten days before my visit the Jap bombers flew over regularly from Lae and Rabaul, but in dwindling numbers. At first they were in groups of twenty to twenty-five, enough to cause severe damage. But now they were satisfied to send over two or three and often only one.

New Guinea taught me the hard facts of air power in the Pacific. There are no airports in the sense we know them at home. When you read about a "Southwest Pacific" airport in the dispatches you should visualize a strip maybe two hundred to three hundred feet wide and a mile long, chewed out of the jungle with bulldozers, and made more or less smooth with flexible steel mats. The average commercial pilot, with thousands of hours of flying in his logbook, would hesitate long before using such a landing field in the United States. But the Air Force youngsters, fresh from the training course, have learned to expect nothing better.

New Guinea is a hellhole of heat, dust, and vermin. I realize that the idea is impracticable, but still I say it would be a good thing for the nation if the top men concerned with labor and war production could be given just one day on that front. There'd be much less chest-thumping about our fine production records. You don't feel like bragging when you see mechanics trying to patch up a $350,000 B-24 four-engine bomber under an improvised shelter of grass and palm leaves. And you don't feel like boasting after you've talked to pilots who are averaging well over one hundred hours of combat flying a month. And that doesn't include uncompleted missions, tests, or practice flights, which add many more flying hours. Yet our men don't complain. They don't complain because they are getting results. When I was there in December they were knocking down four or five Jap planes for every United States fighter lost. This ratio is conservative. It does not include damaged Japanese aircraft, many of which never make their bases.

I flew back to Australia with General Kenney. On the way he stopped to give me a look at a new repair and maintenance depot which we Americans are building some hundreds of miles back of the combat zone. When completed, it will be one of the biggest establishments of its kind in the Pacific. In command of the aviation engineers I discovered a man who had been my first crew chief on the Western Front in World War I, Colonel Victor Bertrandias. Vic told me one of the best stories to come out of the whole trip. A group of United States colored boys were building a landing strip in the Australian desert. Suddenly a kangaroo appeared and because it was the first they had ever seen they set out after him as fast as they could go. Instead of taking to the bush, the kangaroo bounded down the landing strip. After chasing him fifty yards, the colored boy in the lead stopped short and yelled to the others, "Ain't no use chasing him! He ain't let down his front legs yet."

At Brisbane I picked up the B-24 and headed for Guadalcanal. In between I stopped at an air-force headquarters the name of which I cannot mention. Here I fell in with another World War I friend—Major General Millard F. Harmon. "Miff" Harmon, in collaboration with and under the direct command of Admiral William F. Halsey, commands all Army air and ground forces in this key sector, which takes in Guadalcanal, some hundreds of miles away. This island base is the real reservoir of the American air power used in the Solomons. The main repair shops are here, and the fighters and bombers that are warring for control of the Solomons "commute" between the base and Henderson Field. That means hundreds of miles of flying back and forth across the ocean for a few minutes of effective combat flying.

Here, again, they refused to let me go into a combat zone in my unarmed ship. They put me aboard a Flying Fortress which was on a routine search mission. It also acted as navigating ship for half-a-dozen Navy fighters bound for Henderson Field.

Again vast stretches of ocean. Then far ahead I saw a group of islands on the horizon. The pilot nodded— Guadalcanal. That name means to me what I suppose it means to every American. It filled me with pride just to see it.

The Fortress circled over Henderson Field while the fighters landed one by one. I had a good view of the jungle, enough to tell me that its reputation hasn't been exaggerated. Far out to sea the destroyers were patrolling. In my curiosity I stuck my head out the top hatch and in landlubber fashion lost my sun helmet. One of the crew handed me his. "You can have it," he said. "We don't use them up here." I found out what he meant after we landed. Steel helmets are the only headgear worn in Guadalcanal.

I spent only one night and a day on the island. But it was enough to make me mad at myself and my people back home for ever thinking we know what war is. If New Guinea is a hellhole, Guadalcanal is ten times so. The famous Henderson Field which looks so good in the photographs is no field at all; it's just a break in the jungle. Pilots call it "the graveyard." The landing strip on both sides is lined with wrecks—some shot to pieces in the air, others smashed by enemy shells and bombs. The landing strip itself has been bombed and shelled and patched and bombed again so often that to land on it is like trying to land on a roller-coaster track.

It had been raining hard just before we arrived and off the landing strip the ground was just plain mud. A jeep drove up with Major General Alexander M. Patch, of the Army, who had recently taken over command of the ground forces, and his chief of staff, Brigadier General Edmund B. Sebree. They drove me to headquarters, which was just a tent in a gully some distance from the field.

Guadalcanal and New Guinea taught me that war in the Pacific is very different from the kind of war I knew in 1917–18. There are no pleasant leaves in Paris, no châteaux and limousines for the generals. I saw mechanics working in their bare feet. The rainy season was just starting and more than fifty inches of rain will fall upon Guadalcanal before it is over. The dugouts and fox holes were waist deep in water and mud and tents were flooded; everything—tents, clothes, boots—seems to rot away in the damp. Malaria or dysentery sooner or later hits everyone.

They don't stand on ceremony at Guadalcanal. General Patch sleeps on an Army cot in a leaky tent. He wears a regulation jumper with no insignia or ribbons to distinguish him from a buck private. But every soldier and Marine on Guadalcanal knows who he is. That night I had dinner with General Patch in a grass-roofed shack, at a table made of rough planks. Colonel Brooke Allen, head of the bomber force, and Major Harry Brandon, commanding the fighter units, joined us and we went over the immediate and long-range problems.

I certainly make no claim to being a strategist, but I doubt that we shall ever again attempt another operation like the one that has centered on this lone island. It's too costly and tedious. "Guadal" by itself is not worth the life of a single Marine. What we are fighting for, and what the Japs have tried so desperately to regain, is control of that single miserable airfield and the sea supply lines to it. In the long run the cheapest way will be to move in sufficient force to cut through the Japanese string of islands and grab three or four at a time. That kind of operation would give us more airfields to work from, and with plenty of airfields you can assemble striking power fast. And, once established, you can cut to pieces the Jap supply lines to the islands in our rear—provided, of course, we are strong enough to prevent the Japs from doing that to us.

The rain came down in torrents that night. It was a good thing General Sebree showed me to my tent, because I wouldn't have found it in the dark. I missed my footing and went up to my knees in mud. A gas mask and a steel helmet were lying on my cot. I turned in at midnight but I couldn't sleep, partly because of the drumming of the rain on the canvas, partly because of the mosquitoes of which there were billions. The front lines were only a few miles away. Every now and then I could hear the *crump* of the 155's, and occasionally quick bursts of machine-gun fire. But I missed the usual night show. The rain kept away the Jap bombers and the cruisers that usually stand off the beach at night, laying down a well-placed barrage.

Daybreak was welcome because it brought the sun. After a hearty breakfast of wholesome Army rations I packed my sleeping bag, wished my hosts and benefactors good fortune, and started back for the base I had left the day before.

Nothing happened to me on Guadalcanal, but the crew of the Flying Fortress that flew me and six other passengers back had been through plenty. The crew had been out on a violent bombing mission the day before, from which they had returned with only a few bullet holes to show for it. The passengers had not been so lucky. All members of a B-17 crew, they had been out at the same time on a search mission. They ran into fifteen or sixteen Zeros, which ganged up on them. It was a long, running fight back to land. Two of the engines were shot out, the wings, fuselage, and tail were riddled with cannon shot and machine-gun bullets, and the pilot was killed. But they knocked down five of the Zeros, fought off the rest, and brought the Fortress back to Guadalcanal.

Air fighting over the Pacific is just about the hardest kind of fighting there is. It is not uncommon for heavy bomber crews to operate ten or twelve hours at a stretch in hostile air. They are exposed to attack all the way in to their objectives and all the way back. This is the most nerve-racking kind of strain. You must keep a sharp watch above, below, and on all sides. Every cloud holds a potential ambush. The burden is falling upon mere boys—pilots of twenty-two and twenty-three, gunners of eighteen and nineteen.

It wasn't that way on the Western Front twenty-five years ago. A pilot went out to battle like a knight. He was pampered and rested; his every whim was indulged. I can remember patrol after patrol in which I never saw an enemy plane. There was a sort of unwritten understanding that you'd never gang up on a lone airman. If a patrol overtook a straggler, one man would peel off and deal with him on equal terms. Now everybody goes in, on our side as well as theirs.

Let me tell the story of an old friend, La Verne G. Saunders, known throughout the Air Forces as "Blondy." I met Blondy at the base from which I took off for Guadalcanal. He was a colonel then, in charge of the heavy bombardment forces. But I see where they've made him a brigadier general.

Blondy went out on a bombing mission. His airplane was attacked by twenty Zeros. First the copilot was hit in the ankle by a bullet. As Saunders was lifting him out of the seat a shell tore into the copilot's stomach. Saunders laid him on the floor and took the seat. Hardly had he completed this act of mercy when the pilot fell dead over the controls with a bullet through his heart.

The air was full of lead, and the gunners were firing steadily at the Zeros which attacked from all directions. Saunders managed to get the dead pilot out of the seat while holding the plane on an even keel. He then took over the controls. By that time one engine had been badly shot up and in a little while a second one was knocked out. This caused a forced landing on the water near an island north of Guadalcanal.

The rafts were thrown out and Blondy managed to get his crew and the dying copilot off the sinking bomber. They were in Japanese-controlled waters, and Blondy's next problem was to avoid being taken prisoner. Fortunately, the island was occupied by friendly natives, who took them to an Australian "busher." The "busher," who was spying on Japanese movements, had a short-wave radio. He sent word back to Guadalcanal, and a few days later a Navy flying boat stole in, virtually under the enemy's guns, and brought them safely back. The copilot, however, had died; Blondy buried him on the beach.

For sheer guts, untiring effort, and unstinting loyalty to one's men, I can think of nothing to touch that. It is an outstanding example of the kind of leadership our troops are getting. But there are others, many others. I have mentioned meeting my friend General Walker at General MacArthur's headquarters. I should have written the "late" General Walker. On January 11, 1943, a communiqué announced that he was missing in action. He had last been seen over Rabaul, leading a bombing attack. Generals like Ken Walker don't die in bed.

It so happened that the day I left New Guinea I heard General Kenney order him to stop flying in the combat areas. "Ken" objected violently. He said he would continue to fly in combat areas so long as it was his responsibility as a command officer to order young pilots into the fighting. The nation lost a very great officer in "Ken" Walker. He was one of the very few men who fought for the development of the heavy bomber in the early 1920s and the bombing technique which has changed the character of war.

Perhaps it is presumptuous of me to lecture, but I

know what I saw—I was there. A terrible responsibility faces us people back home, a responsibility to which we are not yet fully awakened. Everywhere I went the cry from the troops was for more of everything—more planes, more guns, more tanks, more ammunition, more medical stores. It is hard for them to understand why this rich country cannot send them more.

I have said, and I repeat, that if we were to bring back the troops from the hellholes of the world and place them in the factories, and if we were to take the factory workers and place them in the fox holes, in the filth, vermin, diarrhea, malaria, and Japanese, I will guarantee that production would be increased and in many instances doubled within thirty days. Some have called me a "labor-hater" for saying that. No, I am not a labor-hater. I believe in honest labor unions who are doing their darnedest to turn out the weapons we need. I have been laboring for forty-odd years—since I was twelve years of age—in many lines of endeavor. I come from humble parents. I know the value of honest labor. I have served labor as well as employer. And to those millions of honest men and women war workers go my heartfelt thanks—to those whom, the shoe fits, I say wear it.

My answer is that, after you have seen the stink and corruption of New Guinea and Guadalcanal, after you have come to understand the nature of the enemy, all the talk of social security, old-age pensions, wages and hours, means nothing. We either win the war or we lose it. And we'll lose it if we don't produce.

None of us here is doing so much that he cannot do more. You and I should be grateful for the privilege of doing everything we can.

This trip opened my eyes to one of the great fallacies of our time. In the decade before the war we spent billions on the theory that a superior few could plan the lives and duties of 130,000,000 people. Now we are spending many more billions to inject in our fighting men the qualities of self-reliance, initiative, individuality, and imagination which we had come to deprecate.

Once you put a boy in a fox hole he is on his own. Once you drop a parachute trooper behind the enemy's lines he is on his own. The youth in the cockpit of a fighter, in a tank, on a Commando raid, is always on his own. The "rugged individualist," as a political symbol, may have few friends, but God help us if we can't re-create him on the battlefield and the factory floor.

From the mid-Pacific base I now headed home. An all-night flight put me in Samoa for breakfast. Immediately afterward I went to the hospital to see how Adamson was getting along. To my keen disappointment I found that he had had a serious relapse; he had developed a lung abscess which required an operation. The doctors doubted he could be moved for another ten days. Hans and I tried to greet each other cheerfully, but under the circumstances it was difficult.

However, by the following day there had been an unbelievable improvement in his condition; the doctors said that if I would wait another forty-eight hours, and Hans meanwhile continued to mend at the same rate, they were pretty sure I could take him back to the States with me.

This was good news. In fact, I found good news on all sides. Reynolds had been brought down from Island Z during my absence. He was still very thin and weak, but there was no longer any question of his recovery.

The wait fitted in with my plans because it allowed me to visit a near-by island, also an important Army Air base. I spent the week end with the commanding general. Returning to Samoa Sunday, I went directly to the hospital. Hans greeted me with a big smile—if he had another good night, he could leave with me Monday night. It was one of the happiest moments of my life; Hans had really made a remarkable comeback and I could bring him home in time for Christmas.

And that was the way it turned out. They put an adjustable bed and a cot in the cabin, the first for Adamson and the other for Reynolds. Secretary of the Navy Knox thoughtfully arranged for Commander Durkin, who had been taking care of them, to accompany us back to the States.

We started home Monday night, December 14. Daylight overtook us at a small island, where we breakfasted and refueled the plane. That evening we landed at Hickam Field. So as not to overtax the sick men, we laid over a day before continuing to San Francisco. Sergeant

Reynolds' home was in Oakland and it meant a lot to me to be able to return him to his parents. I went to Los Angeles for an hour's visit with my mother. The airplane, with Hans aboard, picked me up and we flew on to Washington, arriving at Bolling Field December 19, just two months to the day after I left San Francisco.

Mr. Robert Lovett, the Assistant Secretary of War for Air, Lieutenant General Henry Arnold, Major General Harold L. George, head of the Air Transport Command, many other high-ranking officers, Mrs. Adamson, Mrs. Rickenbacker, my sons David and Billy—these and many other friends were at the airport to greet us. It was truly a happy ending. Colonel Adamson, although still in the hospital, is at last off the "very sick" list. All the others have completely recovered. As for Sergeant Alex, it was hard to leave him in the Pacific, but I am sure that he is among friends, and at home.

# CHAPTER V

# Some Recommendations

As a result of the experiences through which we had passed I reached several conclusions as to what should be done about the equipment to make conditions easier for others who may find themselves in our position. This is perhaps as good a place as any to set them down. It seems to me very necessary for the following additions and improvements to be made:

1. That the rafts be made larger, if possible.

2. A silk sheet of appropriate material, four by six, approximately, which could be used as a sail between the crossed oars. This would serve several purposes: It could be used as a shield against the withering sun, and also it would serve as a rain catcher, which is all-important.

3. Concentrated foods in a glass bottle, with a watertight top. (a) Vitamins of the proper kind in the same type bottle. (b) Sedatives of the proper kind to quiet

the nervous system and permit sleep, which prevents the breaking of minds. Should also be in a watertight and airtight bottle.

4. First-aid kit should be in an airtight bottle.

5. Rubber patches and glue should be in an airtight bottle.

6. Flares and Very gun should be protected from salt-water deterioration.

7. Jackknife of medium size, with proper protection.

8. Fishing tackle and some appropriate type of bait, properly protected.

9. All oceanic planes, either combat or transport, should be equipped with a small radio transmitter properly protected to give out proper distress signals and be used as a focal point from which to get bearings.

10. Develop a small salt-water distiller for each raft of three men or more, to purify or distill a minimum of a quart per day.

11. An appropriate steel mirror and smoke bomb, properly protected.

12. All equipment should be properly arranged and housed on the inside of the raft in order to prevent their loss in case of turnover.

13. If possible, the carbon-dioxide tank should be placed on the outside of the inflated roll in order to give occupants more comfort and room.

# Message to America

# Message to America

The UNITED STATES is currently spending thirty billion dollars for aircraft. This is just the cost of the aircraft program. It does not include the pay of the 2,000,000 pilots, navigators, bombers, gunners, meteorologists, and ground crews in the Army and Navy Air Forces; nor does it include the many hundreds of millions of dollars more being spent on airports all over the world. This will provide some idea of the dollar cost of air power in the world today.

When I came back from France after the last war, I was convinced that the airplane had a future that no one could foresee. It could be a wonderful instrument of peace or the deadliest weapon that man had ever created. I had been a successful racing driver, but after what I had learned over the Western Front that no longer meant anything. I had no definite plan, but the one thing I wanted above everything else was to make a career in aviation. The conviction was fixed in my mind that before many years commercial airplanes would be carrying passengers and freight across the ocean, and I thought that was the field for me. It was, of course, partly a selfish ambition. I wanted to be in on the ground floor of a new industry. But the pull went beyond that. Like so many other men who had learned to fly during the war, I had come to believe that the airplane would provide the means for bringing the peoples of the world closer together, for helping them to understand their mutual problems. The air was a natural avenue for ideas and commerce. Even before I left France in 1919 I investigated the chances of making a transatlantic crossing by air. But a survey of the available equipment convinced me that a flight, even on the remote chance that it might succeed, would prove nothing. I came back by boat.

When I look back upon that period I realize how blind we of that generation were. Those of us who fought in the air knew instinctively that the whole course of future wars must change and that the geography of world power was bound to be violently challenged. This was obvious to every man who had flown a fighter or a bomber. But the statesmen of the democratic nations could not seem to grasp the fact, or, if they did, it seemed not to disturb them. Yet I knew this was so; and I wanted to see my own country take hold of this new instrument and develop it for its future safety and greatness.

I worked hard to find a place in aviation. I talked to

many men of great influence in the nation on the subject
of air power. Few were interested and those few did
nothing to prepare the nation. Most of them were down-
right glad the war was over; we and our Allies had won;
our boys were once more safely back in the land they
loved, and they could not bring themselves to believe
that another war would come, at least in their time. As
for air power, they simply could not see it. It was the
province of lunatics and crackpots—and "Billy" Mitchell,
in whose defense I was later to testify.

I therefore went back to the automotive business, and
with the help of friends founded my own company. The
competition was too stiff for a newcomer; in a few years
I lost the company and my shirt. Probably it was a lucky
break for me. The disaster drove me back into aviation.

In 1922, before this happened, I married. My wife and
I went to Europe on our honeymoon. We traveled
through France, England, Italy, and Germany. Thanks
to the reputation that had come to me during the war, I
was able to meet many of the leading statesmen and in-
dustrialists of Europe.

In Germany I came to know many of the famous airmen who had fought so brilliantly on the Western Front.
One meeting I shall never forget. It took place at the
Hotel Adlon in Berlin. Four German airmen called to
pay their respects—Hermann Goering, Erhard Milch,
Vandlent, and Ernst Udet. Two had fought in the
famous Richthofen Flying Circus.

Now my squadron had tangled with the scarlet planes

of the Flying Circus on many an occasion, and I personally had shot down two of the Richthofen aces. But soldiers do not hold grudges; they bore me no hatred. In fact, they greeted me almost like a long-lost friend.

Goering was stout even then, but except as a war hero he meant little or nothing to the German people. The other three also were without importance. The Versailles Treaty had broken up the German air squadrons, and these airmen, or so I thought, had virtually nothing with which to work. Yet all four were rich in a single purpose: to avenge the defeat and restore Germany to power on the continent.

Goering said something I still remember. He said, "Our whole future is in the air. And it is by air power that we are going to recapture the German empire. To accomplish this we will do three things. First, we will teach gliding *as a sport* to all our young men. Then we will build up commercial aviation. Finally, we will create the skeleton of a military air force. When the time comes, we will put all three together—and the German empire will be reborn."

Germany was then caught up in the spiral of inflation. The merchants in the stores and shops had to use revolving price tags on their merchandise to keep up with the constantly declining mark. When I gave the floor waiter and the maid at the hotel fifty marks apiece as a tip, Mrs. Rickenbacker was shocked by my extravagance, but the Germans bowed and scraped and could not find words to thank me. But in American money, our five days at the hotel cost me in tips exactly six cents. Under such circumstances it was difficult to take these German airmen seriously. Germany was a bum among nations. No one worth while had ever heard of Hitler.

In 1935 I returned to Europe. I had just been through the backbreaking job of building and organizing Eastern Air Lines. In addition, the friends of Will Rogers, who that summer was killed in an airplane crash in Alaska, had asked me to head the national drive to raise funds for a memorial to him. Between the drive and my own work I brought myself close to a nervous breakdown. I decided to take a trip to Europe—partly to rest up, partly to have a look at commercial and military aviation in England, France, Italy, and Germany.

On arriving in Paris I got a telephone call from Lord Beaverbrook, publisher of the great *Daily Express* of London and a powerful chain of newspapers. I had first come to know him years before in Toronto where he was plain Max Aitken. Beaverbrook invited Mrs. Rickenbacker and myself to join him for breakfast at the Ritz. The conversation was amiable and aimless, but the thought struck me that Beaverbrook seemed to be more than politely interested in the reasons that had brought me to Europe. He asked me about my itinerary.

"When do you expect to be in England?" he asked.

I looked at my notebook. "Three weeks from this afternoon at four o'clock," I answered.

"Fine," he said. "Could you both have dinner with me?"

In due time I arrived in Berlin. Thirteen years had brought a great change in Germany. Hitler was in power and the country had a new vitality to it; there were no more scenes such as I had witnessed in 1922 when the streets were jammed with frantic people trying to get rid of their marks before another inflationary rise wiped out their savings. Again I met the same four airmen. Goering, blazing with medals, had become Hitler's Number 2 man and chief of the new German Air Force. Milch was his deputy; Vandlent was in charge of highly secret research; Udet was in command of all aircraft production.

"Herr Eddie," said Milch, "remember what we told you in 1922?"

"Yes," I said, "I remember it vividly."

"Well," said Milch, "come and see."

I visited the Junkers factory where 20,000 men, they told me, were working night and day building airplanes. Udet showed me the new Richthofen squadron, which we thought we had driven out of the air. Its headquarters were carefully hidden in the pine woods twenty miles or so from Berlin. I saw with amazement hangars made of concrete and repair shops that were bombproof. There were eighteen planes in the squadron, and it puzzled me that six were merely trainers. "But why trainers?" I asked.

One of the fliers told me boastfully, "We use them to make our clerks, our mechanics, and our kitchen police into fliers. Every squadron in Germany is doing the same thing."

That opened my eyes. The four derelicts of 1922 were assembling a striking force that would shake Europe to its foundations.

My wife and I arrived in London on schedule and went to the Savoy Hotel. An hour later Beaverbrook's secretary arrived with invitations for dinner the following evening at his town house.

The first guest I met was Sir Robert Vansittart, Permanent Undersecretary of State in the British Foreign Office. There were cocktails, but before I had one to my lips Mr. Vansittart led me to a corner, and holding the lapel of my coat, he demanded, "When will 'they' be ready?"

"When will who be ready?"

Vansittart said, "Why, the Germans!"

So that was why I had been invited. Quite a few guests were present, and the discussion was rather hot. I gave it as my frank opinion that "they" would be ready in all probability within five years, and a minimum of three. I based this prophecy not only upon what I had seen of the German factories and airfields, but on the fact that the men then in command of Germany's destiny had been underlings in the last war and knew—or thought they knew—the causes of their defeat. They weren't going to make the same mistakes.

Vansittart nodded his head and in a gloomy tone said that my estimate was too hopeful so far as England was concerned; the Germans would be ready within two years.

I said, "Well, if all Englishmen are as jittery as you are, you can be sure that the Germans know it and they will strike."

Beaverbrook was not impressed. He did not believe it. Neither did my own people. When I returned to the United States I buttonholed many of the high officials of the Army, Navy, and the Government. I told them what I had seen in Europe: the growing strength and purpose of Germany and Italy; the unreadiness of France and England. The Germans and Italians, I said, were going forward, particularly the Germans; a great danger faced us unless we acted at once along certain fundamental lines. For saying that I was called an alarmist and warmonger.

I say now, with neither pride nor satisfaction, that my prophecies were not only fulfilled but exceeded by far. Billions of dollars were spent on useless projects that might well have been used to make the nation strong in the air and on the seas. I am convinced that Hitler would never have struck had we possessed even a small part of the military power that we are mobilizing now.

As early as April 1939, in an article in *Collier's*, I proposed a national program of 50,000 airplanes. Not military airplanes—because of rapidly changing design the value of a combat airplane approaches zero after a couple of years. What I wanted the country to have then was 50,000 transport airplanes. Such a fleet would help us move goods faster; it would bring into being a great national aircraft industry which would be converted quickly in the event of war. Furthermore, it would stimulate the training of thousands of pilots and ground-crew men, who are as indispensable to air power as aircraft. The truth was that we Americans, who talked so glibly about being air-minded, had almost no comprehension of what being air-minded really meant. The press was full of foolish talk about "darkening the heavens" with American planes. Yet the entire air transportation system of the United States was built around less than five hundred commercial aircraft. We did not have a single school capable of training pilots or maintenance men on a large scale. In terms of air power we were a second-class power.

In 1940 Mr. Roosevelt called for what was then considered an enormous program of 50,000 military aircraft. It was clear that we had to set some kind of figure to shoot at, but to me 50,000 did not seem very impressive. From such studies as I had made, I could not see how we could possibly hope to hold our place in the world with less than 250,000 aircraft and pilots, maintenance men, and workers in proportion.

We are all air-minded now. Millions of words have been written on the subject of air power; many extravagant predictions are being made. In many respects the logic of air power has been injured by the foolish claims of its disciples. No man who has made a truly serious study of the strategic situation believes that air power by itself will win the war. It must be used in conjunction with other weapons. But this I believe: the decisive battles will be fought and won or lost in the air. Whichever side controls the air will ultimately control everything. In the great Battle of Britain in the summer and fall of 1940 Goering came within a hairsbreadth of sweeping the R.A.F. from the skies. Had he succeeded, the Luftwaffe would have ruled the air above all Europe. Goering failed, and from that moment on, I am convinced, Hitler lost his great chance to win. The question is: How soon can we build up our own air power, in conjunction with that of Britain and Russia, to smash the Luftwaffe into the ground? Once we smash it, the industrial system—the factories, the railroads, all the communications—will lie exposed to our bomb sights.

The fact that Goering was unable to smash England with his air power has persuaded many Americans that air power at best is an indecisive weapon. If Germany, with all the years of preparation, could not finish off England, how can we expect to finish off Germany with the same weapon?

The answer is that air power has not yet been used in

anything like the concentration required. The compara-
tively small quantities available to ourselves, the British,
and our other Allies, have been dispersed over all the
world. But commencing in the summer of 1943 this situation will change. As the output of the aircraft industry
rises we shall see raids on a scale far exceeding those that
now make headlines. A bombing raid is only an exercise
in transportation. The problem is basically one of moving cargo—in this case bombs—to a specified destination
at a fixed time. We Americans have always understood
transportation; we have led the world in that field. And
in due time we and our Allies shall bring Germany and
Japan under a weight of bombs such as Goering, in his
wild dreams of 1922 and 1935, never visualized.

My visit to Europe in the fall of 1942 gave rise to
certain conclusions which I incorporated in my report
to Mr. Stimson:

My consensus is that American conceptions of Army aircraft and their tactical employment are proving sound in
combat and that the British look upon the practical application of our air war theories with increasing approval.

The trend of the war on the Western Front is clearly one
of air war, and it is my opinion that the European theater
will remain an air theater until we have secured superiority
over the German Air Force and paralyzed the production
capacity of the German aircraft industry.

We have heard a lot of talk in America and a great deal
of misinterpretation of day bombing and night bombing.
Strictly speaking, it is not a matter of day bombing or night

bombing, but day-and-night bombing, with day bombing mainly being devoted to specific objectives, and night bombing aimed mainly on larger areas such as enemy industrial centers. Both types of bombing are important and necessary.

While heavy English bombers can operate in the daytime, they are night bombers mainly. American heavy bombers, on the other hand, can operate in the nighttime as well as in daylight. They have proven, repeatedly, in actual combat, that their speeds, altitude, and terrific defensive fire power make them dangerous game for enemy fighters.

Since American bombers can operate in both daylight and dark, with equal disregard for enemy fighters, and since they can engage in both precision and area bombing, it seems to me that there can be no question whatever that the A.A.F. bombardment theory is well sustained in the crucible of practice.

As for fighter planes, the fog of confusion that existed regarding the respective qualities of American and British fighters is rapidly being dissipated. The fact that American fighter pilots in England flew the British Spitfire was widely misinterpreted in this country as meaning that our own fighter planes were inferior to the Spitfire. That is not at all the case. To begin with, our pilots flew Spitfires in England because Spitfires were available, thus saving the trouble of sending American-made fighter planes to England. Secondly, by using Spitfires in England, we were able to send our fighter planes to other fronts.

Without any quibbling whatever I can say that the British have a strong admiration for both our fighter and bomber types and that they look to the time when the newest types of these planes will be available to English pilots. By this I do not mean to say that our planes are perfect. No plane ever attains ultimate perfection. Warfare, among other things, is a constant battle for superiority in which both sides have only momentary advantages so long as they remain alert and ready to make changes. I have full confidence that the tactical and technical officers in our Air Forces, as well as manufacturers and aircraft designers, realize that quality is a quantity in itself, and that quality is the fruit of constant improvement through constant experimentation.

To this end I strongly recommend that the production head and the engineering head of all American Army combat-type plane manufacturers visit the proper English and American commands in England at least twice a year. This is because changes are so rapid in combat types on both sides that information received in cold print takes too long and loses its importance when it has to be sent from 3,000 to 6,000 miles for interpretation. With such liaison, valuable time would be gained and improvements in development would be materially speeded up.

The United States Air Forces in England are in exceptionally good shape with respect to high command leadership, even down to the group, squadron, and flight leaders. United States Army aviation has a great asset in the fact that virtually all of the senior officers in the various commands and their staffs had extensive experience in World War I and have kept abreast of the times. The effort that is being made here at home toward the careful selection of flight, squadron, and group leaders is paying dividends in England. It is proper that leaders should be developed to the highest point of efficiency before arriving on any front. Never before has leadership played such an important part in aerial warfare.

In the course of my stay in England I visited virtually every fighter and bomber station of the A.A.F. I talked with the members of the air crew and ground crew and found throughout the entire structure the high type of morale that can exist only where men are satisfied with their work, contented with their treatment, and have pride in their equipment. Their general health condition is excellent, the food beyond criticism, and the men are well provided for with respect to clothing.

The understanding between the English and American personnel is exceptionally good from the top down. The English have gone out of their way to welcome the American air contingents and render them every assistance. This applies to the military as well as to the civilian population.

The picture I obtained with respect to the progress of the war on the Western Front is that the trend is entirely in our favor. As far as I could ascertain the total German Air Force does not exceed 4,700 operational combat planes of every type, a very small percentage of these being bombers. It would be a mistake, however, to draw the conclusion that German air power is on the decrease. While we may hope that British and American bombers have crippled German aircraft production and maintenance in Germany and France, the case may well be that the Germans are working feverishly on new-design planes to offset the aerial superiority which, at the present writing, is definitely on the Allies' side.

We are bound to suffer losses, maybe even great losses, before the conquest of Germany is completed. There is no question that we will win this war. The only question is how soon. That question can only be answered by figures of production because the first line of offense is the production line.

In that connection I may point out that our problems with respect to airplane types are behind us. Our bombers have proven their worth with respect to types and tactics. All that remains now is to continue our experiments to improve types now in service and the new heavy, high-altitude bombers that already have left the blueprint stage. The same holds true with respect to fighter planes now in service in England. These include the P-38, the P-51, and the P-39. As for light and medium bombers, the A-20, B-25, and B-26 have also won deserved praise for their highly efficient basic characteristics.

I may add here that the new Spitfire-9 is a great improvement over the previous type of this fighter which saved the day in the Battle of Britain.

While I do not feel at liberty to discuss the progress and production of British planes, I can say that the British are continuing along their established line of long-range night bombers. I see in this a very happy union of British night aerial bombing and American daytime precision bombing which will complement each other into round-the-clock bombardment, in increasing tempo, and extending range as more equipment and personnel become available. In fact, day bombers will be able to serve as pathfinders for night bombers by lighting fires on enemy targets in the daytime— fires which will serve as beacons for the bombers in the night.

As I said before, the picture, from our standpoint, is as bright as the grim portrait of war can be. But let us not be complacent about it. The cancer of complacency is deadly. We must keep our aircraft plants going at full capacity and send a steady stream of bombers, fighters, air crews, and ground crews, and all that goes with them, flowing on to England, so that in time there will be a constant cloud of Allied combat craft over the skies of Germany.

What I saw in the Pacific served to reinforce these conclusions. The fundamental fact is that with troops scattered all over the world, on both land and sea, we are nowhere able to strike effectively unless we first have local superiority in the air.

Japan is a formidable enemy. Her conquests have given her huge sources of materials, which we can be sure she is diligently converting to war. I have mentioned earlier, and again repeat, a conviction which is not merely my own but that of the great majority of officers now fighting in the Pacific: it is that we must not delude ourselves into believing that we can destroy Japan by fighting our way to her industrial heart, island by island. Guadalcanal and New Guinea, which are only two steps out of a thousand, have shown that. The island-by-island procedure would exhaust even our own great resources and tax the country into the next generation. Rich as we are, we cannot afford to gamble that long.

General MacArthur, in a recent statement from his headquarters in the Southwest Pacific, said that the campaign in Papua tested a "new form of campaign which points the way to the ultimate defeat of the enemy in the Pacific.

"The offensive and defensive power of the air and the adaptability, range, and capacity of its transport in an effective combination with ground forces represent tactical and strategical elements of a broadened conception of warfare that will permit the application of offensive power in swift, massive strokes rather than the dilatory and costly island-to-island advance that some have assumed to be necessary in a theater where the enemy's far-flung strongholds are dispersed throughout a vast expanse of archipelagoes. Air forces and ground forces were welded together in Papua, and, when in sufficient strength with proper naval support, their indissoluble union points the way to victory through new and broadened strategic and tactical conceptions."

There are several regions from which we might deliver these "massive strokes."

We could bomb her from China—but that means carrying bombs and repair parts two thirds of the way around the globe. But from Siberia we could bomb Japan just as effectively with perhaps as little as one fifth the investment in men and matériel. But that would require the acquiescence of the U.S.S.R.

No matter how we go about fighting the war with air power, we must steel ourselves for a tremendous investment. I don't see how we can do the job with less than 300,000 pilots, 200,000 combat crews, 100,000 instructors, and more than three million men on the ground. All this for air alone.

This immense establishment will be at our command with the peace, and we must educate ourselves to use it wisely. I have no desire to add another prophecy about the possibilities of postwar aviation. We all know that the possibilities are measureless. In my opinion, the major postwar problem for Americans to weigh is what their stake is to be in the world's air, and how far they will be prepared to go to keep it from ever again becoming a one-way avenue of attack for our enemies.

We face an enormous political decision; we must learn to think of the air as we once thought of the seas and of the great strategic rivers and highways. Our statesmen and the statesmen of our Allies—and in time the leaders of our present enemies—must hammer out a formula that will give all nations free and unhindered access to the new high routes.

More than one hundred years before the Wright brothers flew, an English scientist, Sir George Cayley, said, "An uninterrupted navigable ocean that comes to the threshold of every man's door ought not to be neglected as a source of human gratification and advantage." That advice still makes sense. Americans of this generation will have betrayed their destiny if they let their sovereign rights and responsibilities within that ocean of air slip out of their hands. Unless the statesmen are able to deal with the issues raised by air power, they cannot hope to deal with the old and troublesome institutions underneath. From this day on, I venture to say, there will never be peace if the air is left in chaos.